Purpose

A Personal Coaching Program to gain clarity
what is really important
in your life and
to stay focussed in a changing world

This book is dedicated with gratitude to our parents

Margarete and Heinz Huhn, Hilke and Manfred Backerra

Gerhard Huhn / Hendrik Backerra

Purpose

The Secret of Self-Motivation

*A Personal Coaching Program
to gain clarity
what is really important
in your life
and to stay focussed
in a changing world*

Emergence Publishing

The Authors:

Dr. Gerhard Huhn, Berlin and Hendrik Backerra, Berlin

Copyright © 2008 / 2014 by Gerhard Huhn and Hendrik Backerra
Second Printing 2014

Emergence Publishing Berlin
in cocoperation with Hendrik Backerra Consulting Berlin

Translation: Jan-Christer Janson
Editor: Neil Danby
Type-setting: Gabriele Mammitzsch

ISBN 978-3-9812274-1-3

Books can be many things. So perhaps we should start
by clarifying exactly what it is you are holding in your hands here –
so as to avoid any fundamental misunderstanding from the outset.

As readers we expect suspense or laughter from an author – at best both,
or at the very least entertainment. When it comes to non-fiction, we hope to gain
new knowledge or insights, to be taken into unfamiliar worlds,
or to be given advice on how to deal better with our professional or private lives.

Nothing of the sort awaits you here.
This is not a book for people looking for passive enjoyment
but for those like yourself (otherwise you wouldn't have bought it!)
who are actively taking their lives into their own hands.

We have not written this book as an exciting read,
but instead have tried to imagine ourselves as trainers and coaches,
accompanying you on a wholly personal discovery journey to a life of purpose.

The enjoyment that you can get from this book
will not come from the mere act of reading,
but from involving yourself in the process and exercises it presents.
It is thus an action book in the truest sense of the word.
From the first page onwards a complete, personal training program is presented,
and you are invited to take part in the process it maps out.

We promise only one thing:
If you take the time to do more than simply flipping through the pages
(although doing so may initially threaten to put you off),
if you make the effort to put the suggestions we make into practice,
then you are in for an exciting ride towards a meaningful and purposful life.

When you finish the last page,
you will be a different person from the one who picked up this book in the first place.
Furthermore, we are not limited by space and time in the sense that we are no further
away than the nearest Internet connection: you can reach us via www.mypurpose.de.
Enough said. Let's get started.

But first, we wish you an inspiring journey of discovery!

Gerhard Huhn and Hendrik Backerra
– who look forward to your postcards (or mailings) from the road.

Contents

Part III: Appendices 1–4, Acknowledgment, Authors

Foreword

by Prof. Mihaly Csikszentmihalyi, Ph.D.,
author of FLOW – *The Psychology of Optimal Experience*

When I talk about flow, people often ask: *"What can I do to achieve happiness?"*

To be happy is a universal human desire. So it is not too unexpected that people might think that – after more than 2000 years of philosophy and 30 years of scientific research – a formula for happiness has been discovered, and is ready to be used. But equating flow with happiness is the result of a few misconceptions. The first is that happiness and flow are synonymous. The second is that flow experiences can be created by following a set of rules or a checklist of to-do's.

What I have attempted to do over the decades is to identify the internal and external conditions under which people have optimal experiences: those exciting moments during which their feelings, desires, and thoughts are in harmony, free of conflicts that cause confusion. Their consciousness is centered in the here and now, and they feel that they are doing exactly the right thing at that moment. In my book *Finding Flow*, I wrote: *"These exceptional moments are what I have called flow experiences. The metaphor of 'flow' is one that many people have used to describe the sense of effortless action they feel in moments that stand out as the best in their lives."*

Because feelings, wishes and thoughts, activities or joyful moments of silent contemplation are different from person to person, there are millions of ways to reach this kind of harmony.

Therefore, as I have demonstrated in my books, there is no single way to experience flow. However, individuals who have these experiences often report that certain internal and external conditions can be observed in connection with the feeling of flow. The descriptions of these conditions differ slightly in each of my books. Occasionally I have been tempted to provide a *"recipe for flow"*. But I resisted this; instead, my approach was to whet the curiosity of my readers and listeners to figure out for themselves what set of conditions allow them to achieve flow experiences.

As a result, you will find several answers in my books to the question *"What are people doing when they experience flow?"* But I have never found the time to write a book that could answer the question *"What can I do to experience flow?"* The bridge from my research to day-to-day practice was still missing.

It was not until 2002, when I was asked to read a proof copy of a German book about self motivation, that I realized this missing link had been found. The two German authors, Gerhard Huhn and Hendrik Backerra, managed to write the book that provides a bridge from my research to daily life.

It is my great pleasure to introduce now the English – and updated – version of this book. I recommend it to all those people who have been searching for a practical way to transfer my ideas and findings into action. The book is not a cookbook of easily replicable recipes to follow. With sensitivity to the complexity of what we now know about the *"optimal experience"*, a solid theoretical background, and a straightforward, practical approach, the authors offer step-by-step *self coaching* into the world of flow.

Both authors have worked as consultants, management trainers, and coaches for many years, and the book is a result of their ongoing commitment to integrating the possibilities of flow experiences into the business world. This integration is key to motivating performance from internal forces rather than external factors.

Efforts to provide external motivation are often short-lived, can have manipulative aspects, and may be highly expensive. Power that comes from personal, internal drives is not only sustainable, but also self-energizing. It seems that only a minority of companies have embraced the potential of self-motivation until now.

But the role of flow in business represents only one aspect of this work. This book has been written to meet the personal needs of readers who are looking for orientation and want to live a meaningful life. What makes it very special is the way the concept of flow has been combined with two additional ones: What Viktor Frankl has called the *human search for meaning* on one hand, and the results of more than 30 years of research that the Gallup Organization has conducted in the field of *talents and strengths* on the other.

There is no fast track to achieving flow, and getting there requires time and effort. But the payoff is clarity about what is really important in one's life, rather than lost time walking through a jungle of superficial advice.

This book offers a thorough description of the process of goal-setting and several well chosen, easy-to-follow self-management tools. But it is more: it charts a personal journey for the reader and provides a key to personal mastery. It is based on a clear distinction between flow and happiness, but enables the reader to reach both states of mind. It offers support to all of us who want to live a life of meaning and purpose.

I wish its readers a joyful journey.

Claremont, June 2008, Mihaly Csikszentmihalyi

Mihaly Csikszentmihalyi, Ph.D., is a psychology professor at Peter F. Drucker School of Management, Claremont Graduate University and Director of Quality of Life Research Center in Claremont, California and is the former head of the department of psychology at the University of Chicago.

Instead of an introduction ...

It is not the intention of this book to motivate you as a reader. Adding yet another book to what is already a considerable number of motivational publications would not have motivated us as authors, especially since the available list includes many excellent and highly recommended bestsellers. Moreover, we are certainly not aiming to take issue with the arguments and strategies proposed by any of these. In our opinion, they have their own particular purpose and many can be of enormous help in specific situations in life.

What we wanted to do was to write a book for those readers who are not looking for simple formulas. Our concept here is, above all, to provide information. We want to give our readers the chance to identify the system of urges, drives, and motivations that shape their lives, to find out why their "weaker selves" are sometimes so powerful, and to learn what they can do to overcome the pull of their alter egos and live their lives the way they want to.

> "Anyone who stops learning is old, whether at 20 or 80."
> *Henry Ford I.*

If you make the effort to work through this book, it will yield many rewards. When your energy level is low, it will enable you to pull yourself up by your bootstraps. When you are bursting with energy, it will help you channel this energy in ways that enable you to enjoy life to the fullest.

> "The purpose of life is to live it, to taste experience to the outmost, to reach out eagerly and without fear for newer richer experience."
> *Eleanor Roosevelt*

As long as you live in the hope that a book, a seminar, or a coach can provide you with motivation, you are looking for a dependent relationship. This is not, in itself, negative. Various forms of dependency are a part of life. Anyone who aims to be completely independent is headed for dependency on independence. However, when it comes to the subject of motivation, we need to take a closer look at these issues.

Here we are dealing with the inner source of our drives, with the energies that propel our lives, and the question of how we apply them.

"It is personalities, not principles, that move the age."
Oscar Wilde

Shifting the responsibility for our lives to others is a mistake that often has grave consequences. Michael LeBoeuf characterizes this kind of attitude as follows: *"Other people determine my life. This allows me to take credit for my successes while passing the buck when I make mistakes."* Leboeuf regards it as an innate human failing *"to look outside our own persons for all the reasons we can't do something. Always making others responsible for ourselves leads to frustration for everyone concerned. If other people are determining the course of your life, this is simply because you are giving them the opportunity to do so. Ultimately everyone is responsible for their feelings, triumphs, sense of fulfillment and failures. Accepting this fact represents a giant step forward. Albert Ellis summarizes this brilliantly: 'The best years of your life are the ones in which you decide your problems are your own. You don't blame them on your mother, the ecology or the President. You realize that you control your own destiny.'"*

In our seminars and personal consultations we have seen that many of the motivational approaches on offer are too complicated for most potential users. The result is that people read a book or attend a seminar and then have a bad conscience when they don't get around to putting into action the program they've been shown. The motivation to motivate does not find its mark.

"Everything should be made as simple as possible, but not simpler!"
Albert Einstein

Einstein once said that everything should be made as simple as possible, but not simpler! This is the dilemma. Without a deeper understanding of possible interconnections, motivational self-help books that are too simple prove ineffective because their subject matter is not a technical or methodological phenomenon, but the questions concerning the purpose of life and deeper emotions we all grapple with in life. However, engaging too intensively with the psychological or even philosophical aspects of human existence runs the risk of losing sight of what can be applied in practice. Therefore, we have attempted to make things as simple as possible, but not *too* simple. We have not reinvented the wheel. We have simply drawn together insights from a wide range of fields – aspects of the extensive literature already available in this area – and, above all, our own and others' experiences. We use all this knowledge to chart a path to self-motivation for our readers – a path that not only has a solid foundation, but one that can also be "traveled" in a reasonably brief period of time.

You will quickly realize that this book is not merely meant for reading. You will only *benefit* from what it offers if you *actively participate in the process it describes;* if you bring your own thoughts to bear and use it as a *tool.* We have emphasized the key stages of participation by enclosing them in boxes. And in case you are not comfortable writing directly in the book, feel free to make copies of the relevant pages before beginning the process. If you have access to the Internet, you can also download all the sections you need (plus additional information). We have provided a reference to our website in the margin:

> You can also download the participatory sections of this book from the Internet at: **www. mypurpose.de.**

www.mypurpose.de

We are primarily coaches, not writers. We have put this book together on the basis of our day-to-day work with people looking for meaningful ways to shape their lives.

Primarily, our approach is practical rather than theoretical, so it is quite valid to follow the practical steps and only consult the explanatory sections of the book (or the more detailed material on our website) if you want to know why we have suggested a particular strategy. In any case, we have taken Einstein's cue and restricted our explanatory material to what seems absolutely necessarily.

Enough with opening remarks. Let's get going. Beginnings are always difficult. We are not promising "instant happiness." Improving quality of life and making it more meaningful comes at a price, but anyone prepared to invest the necessary energy will be richly rewarded, with an exciting, satisfying, and challenging life – a life full of happiness, enthusiasm, and inner peace. Before you continue reading, let's go straightaway to a practical exercise.

Why are you interested in this book?

Answer the following questions:

Why am I interested in this book?

What benefits and what advantages should it bring me?

What sort of entertainment value do I expect from it?

How much time do I want to invest in working with the contents of this book?

How thoroughly do I want to read this book?

O I just want to flip through it

O I'm intending to read it carefully

O I will work through the book with a pencil and paper or PC to put its suggestions into practice

O I would like to absorb what this book has to offer well enough to pass on the contents to others

www. mypurpose.de

O I am particularly interested in improving my life in these aspects and areas:

_____

_____

_____

PART I

Focusing Attention

Focus 1: Self-Motivation – locating our sources of energy

"Nothing is more difficult than consistently acting according to trivial insights."　　　　　Anonymous

The chances of our lives being a success, declining into a boring routine, or melting down into a constant struggle with stress, depend crucially on how we deal with three things: energy, information, and time.

Dealing with energy, information, and time the right way.

Above all, it is important that we find a way to deal with these three factors and bring them into harmony with one another. But it is also important to meaningfully coordinate the way we deal with energy, information, and time. To give our lives quality and purpose, we need to pay attention to the quality of our ATTENTION.

Paying attention to the quality of our ATTENTION.

Exhaustion, listlessness, and lack of motivation are warning signals. There is always a reason for a lack of drive in our lives, whether professional or private. Of course, such a lack of drive can have physical causes and it is always wise, as a first step, to have a medical examination if constant exhaustion is a problem. "Burnout" syndrome often requires medical treatment and this book cannot act as a substitute where medical intervention is needed. However, it may support and complement such treatment.

If you want to start the day charged with energy as well as enjoying your private life after working hours, putting into practice the suggestions in this book might turn out to be a decisive step in a whole new direction.

Do you know someone who radiates such a high level of energy that it seems to be "infectious?" Where do people like this get their energy? And yet, if you get to know someone like this, if you study them, it's highly likely you'll find that they have problems of their own, even if this isn't immediately obvious. In fact, such people may have very difficult lives. But if you take the time to closely observe such people you will find that one characteristic becomes increasingly apparent: what distinguishes them from those around them is their ATTENTION.

ATTENTION

Drifting through life, not paying attention to what is happening around us, rapidly drains our energy. Information floods our minds, confuses us, and we never seem to find the time to really identify the things that we want to achieve.

The connection between self-motivation and focused ATTENTION.

Primarily, self-motivation means simply gaining access to the energy that drives our actions and learning to direct and focus this energy. In other words, we must first mobilize the willingness within ourselves to act before we can hope to achieve the results we are aiming for. This orientation, this focusing of our interests, leads us to focus our ATTENTION.

ATTENTION is generated if something interests us or if we are confronted with a situation (e.g., danger) that compels us to focus our senses on a specific event (e.g., the approach of a car).

"Advertising may be described as the science of arresting the human intelligence long enough to get money from it."
Stephen Butler Leacock

Of course, in principle, where we direct our ATTENTION is our own choice, but it is important not to forget that we live in a world where billions are spent on directing our attention. We are constantly threatened with a loss of control over where we direct our ATTENTION. Thousands of companies and dozens of TV stations strive to catch our eye. An endless range of films, books, journals, magazines, newspapers, radio broadcasts, games, videos, DVDs, and CDs are produced that only provide their producers with profits if they can manage to attract the ATTENTION of a sufficient number of people. Then there is your boss, or if you are the boss, your colleagues and your customers, who expect ATTENTION from you; and your wife or husband, your friends, your children, parents, grandparents, fellow club members, the list goes on. The whole world around you fights, struggles, begs, pleads, or quietly hopes for your ATTENTION. They do this in ways that are naive or clever, fair or unfair, effective or, often, in vain. They begin doing this as soon as you open your eyes and continue until you close them to recover by getting a little sleep.

Don't misunderstand what we are saying here: the efforts of other people to gain our ATTENTION are not a bad thing. Everybody pursues their own legitimate interests. We can always decide for ourselves if we want to pay ATTENTION to what is dangled in front of us. The point is that we should do this based on deliberate decisions, not on subconscious reactions. It may be meaningful and enjoyable to give our full attention to a novel advertisement and to become interested in an appealing product. In a similar way it might be nice to spend time with friends, even if the day in question has been set aside for gardening work. However, we can use this second example to illustrate a very important point: we should make a deliberate decision and then do things with our whole heart. We need to enjoy the company of our companions without our minds drifting to the subject of weeds and snails!

The fact that other people can attract our ATTENTION is based on our genetic and mental make-up, which makes us easy to distract. Our limbic system (a part of our brain that is located below the cortex) generates powerful impulses that compel us to seek pleasure and try to avoid unpleasant experiences. These impulses are often much stronger than the signals from the cortex. (If you are looking for the source of those "baser instincts" you want to overcome, then the limbic system is a good place to start.) The cortex, with all its intelligence, is still not the "boss" of our minds!

Limbic system: see glossary.

Self-Motivation through an awareness of the capacities of our brains.

The more others are able to understand how we can be influenced, the easier it is for them to ensure we devote time to their interests. Companies and advertising agencies spend large amounts of money on developing sophisticated concepts for acquiring customers and motivating them to buy their products or use their services.

A prerequisite for self-motivation is, therefore, the ability to block the attempts of all those who are trying to manipulate us in their own interest, and to locate our own inner strengths, interests, desires, and values. Enhancing one's own energy thus entails:

1. Becoming aware of the potential "energy thieves" in our surroundings.

2. Applying our energies in a fully aware way.

"The brain is an organism for resisting unwelcome new experiences."
Peter Sloterdijk

In fact, our brain is well prepared for this task. The german philosopher Peter Sloterdijk once described the brain as *"an organism for resisting unwelcome new experiences."*

In effect this means that we *only* pay ATTENTION to *new experiences that are welcome* while not (consciously) perceiving unwelcome ones. However, the criteria that define what is welcome are not something we normally give much thought to. Such criteria tend to be irrational and arbitrary, and are often based on preferences and dislikes formed when we were much younger. High time then to check whether these selection criteria are compatible with the life you want to lead. What is it you focus your ATTENTION on? What kind of information has a chance to enter your mind? Do you retain the things that are *really* important to you? Are you actually aware of what is important to you? What sort of new experiences are welcome? What do you want to experience and how do you want to live?

Or do you live a life that is mainly determined by what other people in your environment (in the past or present) see as important?

Shield yourself from manipulation and motivation by others.

Shielding yourself from attempts by others to manipulate you and strengthening your own motivation are easier if you understand some of the causes that make us do or not do things. Previously, issues such as these were addressed primarily by philosophers; however, for the last hundred years or so it has been, above all, psychologists who have produced concepts aiming to help explain the causes and motives behind our actions. Research over the last hundred years has produced a range of theories, and indeed it may be that the complexity of the human mind is better described by a variety of explanations rather than a single, clear model. Whatever the case, we would like briefly to present a number of fundamental aspects of this research to provide a "foundation" for the very practical work, which will then follow.

But before continuing, we would like you to try a short exercise, and to focus on a few guiding thoughts as a way of preparing yourself for the work that lies ahead:

First preliminary consideration: We never start with nothing …

Thinking about the future, considering what should be, usually also means considering what should change. In this case, your attention that you lack, to things you wish or strive for. This can give rise to a great deal of dissatisfaction and negative feelings that can, in turn, have a paralyzing effect and stifle your drive because your ideas seem unreachable or the absence of something important dominates your thinking.

Therefore, it is useful first to construct a positive emotional base, a feeling of self-confidence. Take some time to appreciate what you have already achieved.

Thus, before you deal with the opportunities for shaping your future, we advise you to take a little break and consider what it is you already have.

> Please note – whenever you see this symbol in the margin you should stop reading and **become active**. Use the following short exercise to train your self-discipline in this respect. You or the person who gave you this book has paid a lot for it. If you want to increase its value for you, **reading is not enough. You have to act.**
>
> Not tomorrow, not sometime soon. **NOW!**

All exercises can also be down-loaded from our Internet address: **www. mypurpose.de** and printed out for your personal use.

At the beginning of the following exercise, concentrate on the things you can already be thankful for. Take a few minutes to congratulate yourself on the things you have already achieved. How about a relaxing cup of tea or a glass of water? Surely you have some music you can put on that inspires you and enhances your good mood. Get something to write – we'll wait for you. Now, take some time to remember:

What successes, triumphs over previous limitations, and experiences of achievement can you remember?

What are your strengths, your particular abilities? What activities and situations make you feel good and at one with world?

Where and when do you find you have particular stamina? Where and when have you been able to infuse others with your enthusiasm?

What have you been praised for? What have you received particular recognition for?

What have you learned?

What sort of tests have you passed?
(You may want to include a swimming or a driving test here. Do you recall how exciting it was at the time and the degree of effort you made?)

What have you already achieved?

What are the things about yourself that you value?

What gifts have you been given?

Are there situations and moments in your life you feel you can be proud of? Have you been brave in a difficult situation? Have you shown civil courage? Have you ever had extraordinary (perhaps even undeserved) luck?

What moments of genuine happiness have you experienced in your life?

In which moments did you feel meaning and purpose in your life?

Are there particular strengths, talents, and abilities you have inherited or developed early, which you can easily call upon and which provide you with a feeling of certainty in particular areas of your life?

Second preliminary consideration: The trap of "everything or nothing."

Before we begin the process of self-motivation, we want to emphasize two further aspects:

Abraham Maslow, who researched the secrets of human motivation as competently as very few other psychologists, pointed out that people create lots of unhappiness in their lives by undervaluing, sometimes even rejecting the things they have already achieved. In such cases, goals that have been reached lose their meaning and only the things that have not yet been reached remain important.

"The attempt to be perfect causes much pain."
Melodie Beattie

Another trap that leads to unhappiness is the tendency toward unrealistic perfectionism – our desire for perfect people, a perfect society, perfect teachers, parents, politicians, the desire for a perfect job, the perfect lover, friends who accept us without restrictions, and generally for permanent, ecstatic happiness. Such expectations are illusions that automatically lead to disappointments, disillusionment, and, according to Maslow, also to *"disgust, anger, depression and a need for revenge."*

The trap of "everything or nothing."

Anyone who falls into the trap of *"I either get everything or I want nothing"* is deprived of the chance to choose between better or worse.

We would like to encourage you to choose between real options instead of dreaming of building castles in the air.

It is a path to health. Maslow writes:

"Health is an achievable reality."
Abraham Maslow

"Healthy persons exist, although their number is small. It is therefore proven that health with all its associated benefits is possible, is an achievable reality. To all people who prefer to see instead of closing their eyes, who prefer to feel good instead of bad, to be whole instead of crippled, it can be recommended that they strive for psychological health.

Knowing that such wonderful people can and do exist – even in a small number and on feet of clay – is sufficient to give us courage, hope, strength and trust in ourselves and our possibilities of growth. Hope for human nature, however limited, should help us on the path to brotherly love and empathy."

The findings of researchers

What in fact is "self-motivation"?

The word self-motivation contains the word *"motive"*, which has its root in the Latin words *"motivum"* or *"motivus"*, which are related to *"movere"*, the Latin word for *"moving"*. A popular dictionary defines motive as *"inducement"* (*a condition that leads to a certain reaction or behavior of a person*). *"Motivating"* is defined as *"inducing somebody to do something"*.

A brief definition of motivation: The energy that mobilizes "I want to" and "I will" and "I can".

The Duden dictionary describes *"motivation"* as *"the total of all inducements and influences that affect an action or similar event."* Others define motivation more cautiously as *"the readiness for a specific behavior and the probability of its occurrence"* (Bertelsmann Lexicon).

"As long as people live and act, they have to follow some sort of plan."
Georg A. Miller,
Eugene Galanter,
Karl H. Pribram

In simple terms, motivation mobilizes energy and puts us in a position to implement our plans, or those of others.

It makes us say *"I want to"* and *"I will"* and *"I can"*.

Human beings are planners. Everything they do or decline to do is associated with certain prior ideas or internal images of the desired state. Many, most likely even the majority of these scenarios, do not reach our conscious mind. There are numerous processes in our mind to which the conscious part has no or only limited access.

This is often overlooked. In daily language we use words such as *"plan"* or *"goal"* only for future states that we consciously aspire to. However, sometimes sub-conscious "plans" prevent us from reaching the goals that we have consciously set for ourselves.

Take, for instance, the case of a person who decides to place a photo of their partner and children on their work desk in order to maintain and deepen their link with them during the working day. If the feelings that generated the idea are strong enough, this person will develop the necessary level of energy to select or take a suitable photo, to have it enlarged to the right size, to buy a picture frame, and to place it on the desk. However, if during this process life at home becomes stressful, motivation might be decreased and cause the person to abandon the whole idea at the first sign of an obstacle (there is no suitable photo, no parking place can be found in front of the picture-frame shop, etc.). In this case, the energy invested was not strong enough to realize the intention. Alternatively, the idea of placing a photo on one's desk might, in itself, increase the level of affection between the person and their family. Selecting a photo with the respective partner could well bring back memories of an especially pleasant holiday, which in turn reignites certain romantic feelings, with the result that the person makes an extra effort and arranges for a new family picture to be taken by a professional photographer.

The tricky thing about motivation is that its practical context often involves situations that are not clearly structured, where a range of different emotions, needs, drives, motives, and energies simultaneously struggle to assert themselves within us.

Anyone who doesn't know where he wants to go shouldn't be surprised when he arrives at a quite different place.
Popular saying

From motivation to motivating

Motivation research attempts to identify the sources of the energy that drives the following process:

> **Goals** and **tasks** are realized via appropriate **measures** and **resources** and lead to the desired **result** – and thus, to **success**. The drive needed for the successful negotiation of the steps involved comes from the **energy** of the individual and a **focusing of emotions** that orientates our ATTENTION to the achievement of the goal. **The source of this emotional drive and ways of concentrating it are the subject of motivation research.**

A new, well-grounded approach: Dietmar Hansch's psychosynergetics

Now, at the beginning of the 21st century, the psycho-energetic model formulated by Dietmar Hansch seems to offer, on the one hand, something truly new. On the other hand, with Rheinberg we have the opportunity of integrating a wide range of different approaches on a scientifically based level. He also explains, among other things, the meaning of those parts of our motivation that we are not consciously aware of, as well as those aspects influenced by our will (see from page 27 onwards).

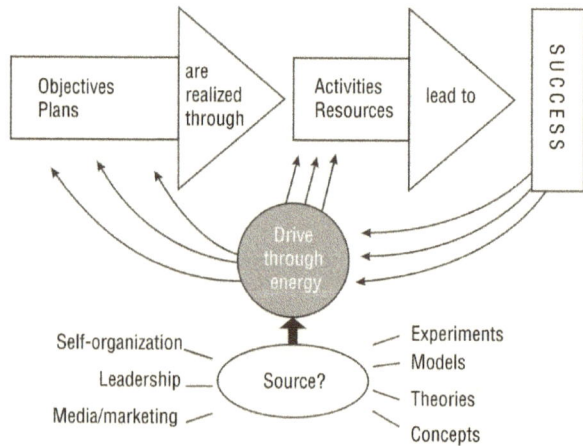

Figure 1: Subjects of motivation research (A) (see also page 26)

Following the dominance of the drive and depth psychology of Freud, Adler, Jung, and others in the early part of the 20th century, a new approach began to emerge in the study of psychology, which had its roots in the response to the introduction of extreme division of labor in assembly line production (Taylorism). From around 1950 onwards, this approach found various expressions in research into the so-called "humanization of labor."

Motivation research thus became the investigation of the lack of motivation and often aimed at answering the question: "How can motivation be generated in members of companies and organizations if it is lacking?" The findings made in this area might seem a promising source of ways to increase self-motivation.

The mistake of taking poorly motivated people as a basis for explaining motivation.

However, this could also be a trap. If a lack of motivation is investigated in a company (which may lead to increased sick leave, decrease in performance, inner resignation, etc.) it is very likely that the researchers will use theoretical models different from those used to investigate the enormous motivational strength of top athletes, mountaineers, entrepreneurs, committed staff members in companies and organizations, researchers, artists, teachers, and therapists (to give only a few examples).

It makes more sense to learn from highly motivated people. Motivational strength rather than motivational weakness needs to be the subject of research. *("Positive Psychology")*

Nevertheless, there are a number of well-known motivational models, which are based on research into ways and means of using *"human creativity completely for the commercial goals of an enterprise"* (McGregor), and which have exerted a considerable influence on our everyday understanding of motivation.

In his book *The Myth of Motivation* Reinhard Sprenger argues that all these motivation theories are based on a pessimistic, negative image of people, which assumes that people on their own are not prepared to work to their full capacity. Therefore, it is the task of management to generate the necessary motivation in order to close these performance gaps. This reduces the problem of motivation to the tension between the interest of

"The system of motivation is mistrust made into a method." *Reinhard K. Sprenger*

the employers, who want to make maximum use of the labor of the employee, and the interests of the employees, who want to *"minimize their effort and the long-term wear and tear on their ability to work while generating the material basis for their own lives, which take place outside the sphere of work"* (Holzkamp/Osterkamp).

Sprenger emphasizes the difference between the (manipulative) efforts of management (*"motivating"*) and the actual (*"intrinsic"*) motivation that develops autonomously. It is a differentiation that we generally support.

Self-Motivation

Let us leave external motivation aside and focus our attention on self-motivation. What interests us here is achieving a healthy state of being, identifying things that we enjoy and which also strengthen us and inspire us to do useful things.

Abraham Maslow | In the 1950s, Abraham Maslow formulated his extended, holistic model of the human being, which he saw as necessary to overcome the narrowness of contemporary psychological models based either on Freudian psychoanalysis or on behaviorism. At the beginning of his major work *Motivation and Personality* he states that his aim is to compare the psychological models formed in the context of therapeutic work with a model of the healthy individual (although he admits that such a model of health is more an ideal than a reality.)

"It will be impossible to understand human life without taking its highest ambitions into account. Growth, self realization, striving for health, identity and autonomy, the desire for excellence (and other forms of striving upwards) now must be accepted as a widespread, possibly universal human tendency."

Principle of
the change
of importance | Maslow argues that we have inborn needs that are structured into a hierarchy of priorities. Once the needs at one level have been satisfied, the needs at the next level gain priority (*the principle of the change of importance*). If, for example, physiological needs such

as hunger and thirst are satisfied, the need for security, which is located at the next level, gains priority and demands satisfaction. Subsequent needs, in order of priority, are belonging, love, recognition and finally self-realization. And at the top of the hierarchy of needs, on the sixth level, is the need for "transcendence". According to Maslow, this highest level represents the human desire to achieve something more than self-realization, to find an identity that is beyond individual human existence.

Hierarchy of needs

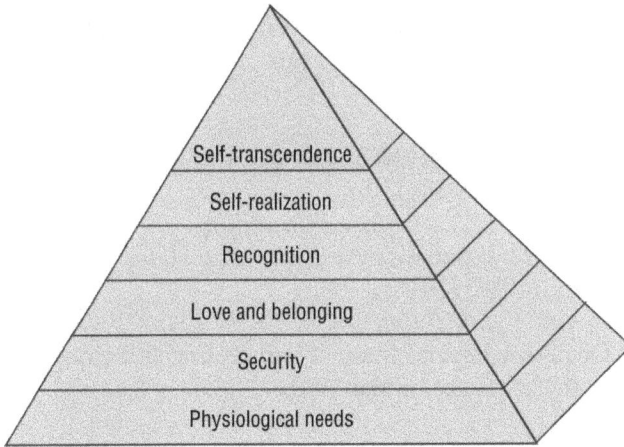

Figure 2: Simplified model of Maslow's hierarchy of needs

For most people even self-realization remains at best a hope or a goal, something that they want and towards which they strive. A few people, however, seem to come much closer to achieving this goal than others. (And of course we all know that all too many people still have to struggle every day just to satisfy their needs for sustenance and security.)

"We cannot live from hope alone – but we cannot live without it."
Lothar Schmidt

Maslow describes the characteristics of self-realizing individuals in a list of 15 points.

15 Characteristics of self-realization

Characteristics of a self-realizing individual

1. Better relationship to reality/greater capacity to deal with uncertainty/insecurity than others.

2. Acceptance of self and recognition of others – and all their peculiarities.

3. High degree of spontaneity (without being extremely unconventional).

4. Problem-centered instead of ego-centered.

5. Temporary need to spend time alone (distanced/objective point of view).

6. Relative independence of environment/culture – without using this as a means of drawing attention to oneself.

7. Appreciation of the important things in life (also those in daily life).

8. Mystical experiences (e.g., ecstatic states, opening of unlimited spaces).

9. Developed social interest and feeling of belonging to the whole of humankind.

10. Deep and satisfactory relationships with people.

11. Democratic views, respect of all people, irrespective of race, religion, and income.

12. Clear separation between goal and path/means; ability to enjoy the process of pursuing goals in itself.

13. Sense of humor, without hostile tendencies.

14. Individual creativity, ability to generate something genuinely new.

15. Ability to resist, where necessary, the demands of culture and environment.

Caution with the image of the pyramid!

Although the image of the pyramid has an appealing symmetry, it is important to bear in mind that it is a simplified representation of what are, in fact, far more complex concepts. However, it allows us to illustrate several basic points in the limited space we have available here.

Two aspects of this image are decisive. First, based on his observations, Maslow argues that humans strive to attain certain states according to a *hierarchical principle* (although this takes place within a complex and dynamic matrix of interconnections and developments).

Second, the importance of goals quickly diminishes once they have been fulfilled to a relatively high degree. At this point new needs quickly become more important and attractive, often to the surprise of the person concerned (*principle of the change of importance*).

Writing around the same time as Maslow, Victor Frankl developed a psychotherapeutic concept that gives priority to the pursuit of purpose and meaning, thus distinguishing his work from approaches emphasizing the central role of needs. (This brought him into conflict with Maslow and initiated a spirited discussion be-tween the two researchers that – at least at the level of self-realization – led to a possible integration of the two approaches.) Frankl describes the pursuit of mean-ing as an independent source of motivation, which triggers actions independent of physiological needs (not only at the top hierarchy level as proposed by Maslow).

Viktor E. Frankl

The pursuit of meaning as a distinctive and fundamental source of drives

In his book Meaning-oriented performance motivation and staff leadership Walter Böckmann, a student of Frankl, dealt in particular with the motivational aspects of this concept and its implementation in the economic and work environment. His thesis is that *anyone who demands performance in the work environment must ensure that the work itself is meaningful.*

"Anyone who demands performance in the work environment must ensure that the work itself has meaning."
Walter Böckmann

It is important to emphasize here that meaning is in the eye of the beholder. Meaningful work is work that has meaning or value for those actually doing it.

Self-motivation means concentrating on things that we find meaningful, that have value, that are important to us.

At the end of our brief tour through motivational research we thus find ourselves back at our starting point: self-motivation means concentrating on things that we find meaningful, that have value, that are important to us. Moreover, the research discussed above suggests **that we can only experience our life as meaningful if we look beyond our immediate, concrete environment and the satisfaction of the needs of our physiological system,** however important these needs may seem.

We can only access the sources of power deep within us if we grow beyond ("transcend") ourselves through:

Three possibilities of experiencing meaning and purpose

- Dedication to a productive activity

- Living for another person or several other persons

- Finding a new attitude to given situations that we might not be able to change or influence

Self-motivation = values-based self-organization

We have to give our lives purpose, and purpose results from realizing values. Values may mean valuable relationships to people, valuable interactions with things, social or individual experiences, or emotions. The direction of our attention towards the realization of values, in terms of personal feelings or experiencing something meaningful, thus offers us a first possibility of recognizing our own sources of self-motivation.

Overview: Part I: Focusing Attention

Focus 1: Self-motivation: Locating the sources of your energy

The first part of this book outlines the process of identifying the types of "lenses" we need to "filter" our attention, because directing our attention involves a whole range of ways of seeing. Sometimes we will have to focus our ATTENTION, as we are doing now, and at other times we might require a lens that *extends* and disperses our point of view.

Fokus 1	Fokus 2	Fokus 3	Fokus 4
Focus 1 Self-motivation – Locating the sources of our energy	Focus 2 FLOW – The pursuit of happiness	Focus 3 Values – Recognizing the forces that drive us	Focus 4 The Goal Scenario – The concentration of forces

The path through part I:
Our lens
for focusing
your attention

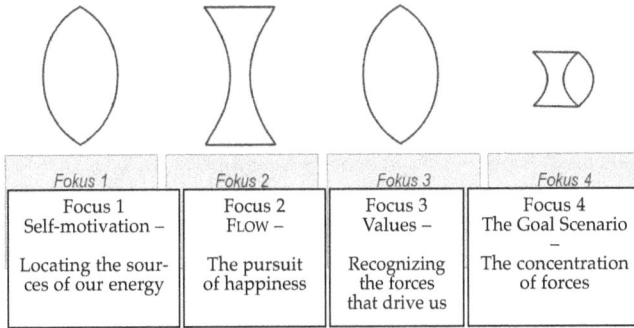

Figure 3: Focusing ATTENTION

Mihaly Csikszentmihalyi, a researcher who has spent the last decades investigating people's search for the experience of happiness, provides us with one such "lens." Formerly a professor of psychology at the University of Chicago, he now occupies a chair at the Peter F. Drucker Graduate School of Management at Claremont University. In the next chapter we will draw on his work to widen our view and to consider the diverse spectrum of human experiences of purpose and happiness. In the third chapter we will concentrate on several especially important values, and in the fourth chapter we will deal with their realization within the framework of a specific Goal Scenario.

Focus 2: FLOW –
The Quest For
Happiness

The Pursuit Of
Happiness

Focus 3: Values
Focus 4: The Goal
Scenario

In the second part of the book we focus our ATTENTION on the implementation of our plans, strengthening our will-power, letting go, trusting, and the process of over-coming internal and external obstacles. Whatever you gain in terms of clarity and motivation is only worth something if it is applied concretely in the here and now. As the German author and humorist Erich Kästner once remarked: *"Good can only come from doing good deeds."*

Part II: Making
Ideas Reality

Energy 1:
Activating willpower

Energy 2:
Overcoming
external obstacles

It seems clear that the drives referred to above moti-vate us to behave in ways that are not purely deter-mined by needs. Such behavior should be understood as belonging to a sphere that has developed out of and beyond the sphere of primary needs, and which has taken on its own specific quality. As a result, this sphere exhibits different behavioral principles to those we find connected with the satisfaction of primary needs.

Energy 3:
Resolving
emotional
resistance
Energy 4:
Resisting the
appeal of urgency

Energy 5: Mastering the day

Two different motivational systems

We can now supplement Figure 1 (page 16) by extending the primary drive area to include an additional, secondary level, in which motives develop that are connected with our pursuit of happiness, meaning, transcendence, and the kind of flow experiences we will be exploring in the next chapter (see Figure 4 on page 26).

The primary system provides for survival and the satisfaction of our needs.

The secondary drives do not only strive for satisfaction but also for enforcement and optimization.

On closer inspection of the secondary drive system, through Dietmar Hansch (he chose to call his concept *"Psycho-Synenergetics"*), an intriguing difference emerged. The primary system mainly seeks to create situations and to obtain certain objects that we aim to achieve, hold, and preserve. Throughout evolution they have proven to aid our survival, and through targets and benchmarks, we can recognize them both physically and mentally. The secondary system seeks to optimize processes. Thus, in the primary system, drives may vanish when targets are achieved. **In the secondary system, however, a drive will be reinforced when the feeling of achievement pushes us, yet again, to accomplish a skill** (e.g., when learning a language, a computer program, a musical instrument, or to play a sport).

Positive Psychology

"Positive Psychology" has been dealing with these aspects of the secondary system since the 1990s. Its distinctive characteristic is it is oriented to the future. In this sense, it contrasts with many other approaches, which remain focused on the past and are strongly influenced by behaviorist concepts and the stimulus-response mechanisms that shaped many of the psychological paradigms of the 20th century.

Dietmar Hansch's work (see bibliography) is a recent example of an approach that looks far beyond previously dominant research concepts.

While our own approach is the result of the interaction between, on the one hand, practical experience gained from more than 30 years of coaching and training and, on the other, the evaluation of academic research, the concepts developed by Hansch form a key element of our theoretical foundation.

"The level of primary, biological motivations is only one layer of the human personality, which is overlaid by a layer of culturally determined secondary motivations. The more we develop our secondary motivations, the more we are able to transcend our nature."

Dietmar Hansch in *Evolution und Lebenskunst*

Sow a thought and you will be able to harvest an action; sow an action and you will be able to harvest a habit; sow a habit and you will be able to harvest character; sow character and you will fulfill your destiny.
Anonymos

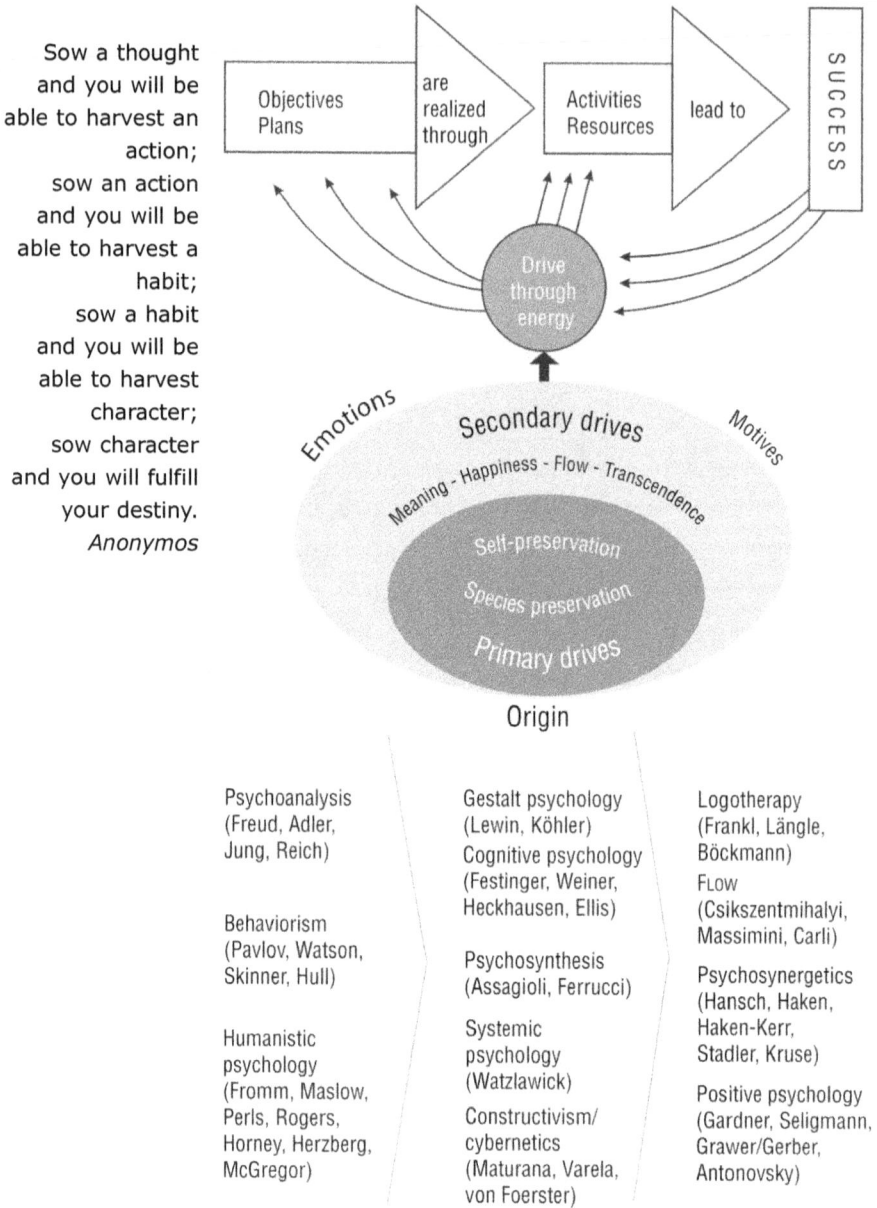

| Objectives Plans | are realized through | Activities Resources | lead to | SUCCESS |

Drive through energy

Emotions   Secondary drives   Motives

Meaning - Happiness - Flow - Transcendence

Self-preservation

Species preservation

Primary drives

Origin

Psychoanalysis (Freud, Adler, Jung, Reich)	Gestalt psychology (Lewin, Köhler)	Logotherapy (Frankl, Längle, Böckmann)
	Cognitive psychology (Festinger, Weiner, Heckhausen, Ellis)	Flow (Csikszentmihalyi, Massimini, Carli)
Behaviorism (Pavlov, Watson, Skinner, Hull)	Psychosynthesis (Assagioli, Ferrucci)	Psychosynergetics (Hansch, Haken, Haken-Kerr, Stadler, Kruse)
Humanistic psychology (Fromm, Maslow, Perls, Rogers, Horney, Herzberg, McGregor)	Systemic psychology (Watzlawick) Constructivism/ cybernetics (Maturana, Varela, von Foerster)	Positive psychology (Gardner, Seligmann, Grawer/Gerber, Antonovsky)

Figure 4: Subjects of motivation research (B)

Next to his differentiation by *psycho-synergetics* into primary and secondary systems, Falko Rheinberg, professor emeritus of psychology in Potsdam, points our attention to further aspects of differentiation in his book *Motivation*. They are individually different and are caused by the fact that even before an infant acquires its speech, basic (*"basal"*) motivational structures are being formed. Regarding the number of these needs, they are few, universal, and probably, evolutionary and biologically developed (e.g., performance, power, closeness to fellow human beings, competition, intimacy, etc.) and the individual person is, as a rule, *not aware of them*. Resulting from these are behavioral effects that are long-term and tend to show through especially in unclear situations – triggered off by momentary impulses. We recognize the effects emotionally – to put it very simply – by feeling good as soon as they are successful and bad when they cannot be achieved.

Some very strong motivational structures develop even before the acquisition of speech (basal motives).

Research on these motivations is still only beginning, and it refers to findings made when using images that allowed for different interpretations. Guided fantasy journeys and the psychological concept of Kathathyme Imagination (or Affective Imagery) (see *Katathymes Bilderleben* by Leuner) also suggest deeply hidden motives, which – according to Hansch's system – are to be associated with the primary system.

Basal motives *can* correspond with those motives that come along at a later stage and are, at that point, linguistically comprehensible for us. However, they can also stay hidden.

As we are acquiring our speech, and also afterwards, the so-called "self-attributed motives" are formed. They are the motives and values that we are aware of, that we already know, or are able to recognize. They are verbally represented and we can name the motives and values, and, therefore, we can describe them to others via our left-hand, verbal half of the brain. In principal, their number is unlimited (unlike the rather straightforward and small number of basal motives). Their individual differences are also considerably more pronounced and they are strongly socially influenced as they are learned. We become aware of them by self-reflection and by analysis (for example, by using the value lists as proposed in this book), however, their behavioral effects are definitely short-term and can, if necessary, be intentionally reactivated (arising from this are, among other things, the meanings of written and pictorial Goal Scenarios, see page 103ff.

By referring to, among others, D.C. McClelland, Rheinberg emphasizes the meaning of differentiating the basal motives from the individual's motivational pictures. The scientist, who is known to formulate his conclusions rather reservedly as well as carefully, describes this differentiation as an *"almost revolutionary assumption."*

Basal motives, however, can also have a conflicting relationship with conscious motives and can, therefore, hinder or even block them.

In any case, today's level of knowledge leads towards the assumption *"that these two motivational systems are completely independent from one another"* (Rheinberg). Indeed, when two independent motivational systems exist there is at least the possibility of them not always aiming for the same goals, and perhaps, from time to time, that they even follow very conflicting directions. Might this lead us to the solution as to why certain goals can only be realized by extreme willpower and sometimes even not at all?

What does this research mean practically? First of all, it appears even a little eerie: There are motivational themes and inner drives that stay disguised to our rational selves, but at the same time, affect our behavior. And we can recognize their effects only as diffuse emotions. We act in a certain way and are unable to explain to ourselves, or to others, why we do certain things (or why we don't). Moreover, it is very conceivable that both motivation systems do not follow the same motives cooperatively, but possibly, by competing, create conflict and hinder or even block behavior. Colloquially said, (and adapted by part of the relevant literature) we are probably tracking down our *"weaker self."*

Be aware of your own feelings and choose goals not only by following values that you are aware of.

In fact, with some of the research participants, the values and motives assumed from the guided fantasy journeys or picture interpretations stood in clear contrast to those that were stated going through the processes of self-recognition. More often than anticipated by the researchers, individuals pursued goals set by themselves without them being in harmony with their basal motives. It is especially people who are very aware of the question of choosing the right goals that are in danger of concentrating merely on cognitive and rational motives. And when the goals do not have the respective basal and emotional foundation, it will make their lives very difficult.

Examples:

The (hidden) basal motive "competition" – meaning to be better than others, to want to beat others – stands in antagonistic contradiction to the consciously named value "teamwork." A person carrying such a constellation of motives within themselves will act consciously in a cooperative, communicative and fair way. However, should a situation become more stressful, or a project be about to fail because, due to long discussions, deadlines are being missed, this person will take over the situation and actively make sure that they do not get into a losing situation. Other team members' needs and considerations become instantly unimportant and will be dismissed. Another example would be an individual whose close contact to family members and friends is a very important basal motive. This person may fight for months in order to get an overseas position within his company because, on a conscious level, it is important to develop their career. As soon as they are told, however, about achieving their promotion their initial euphoria will start to evaporate later the same day. A restless night will follow, many concerns will suddenly arise, major inner tensions will build up, and finally, they will even decline the promotion. For those who believe in even stronger powers of the subconscious, an explanation can possibly be found for when, in an extreme scenario, this person ends up in hospital following a sports accident one week before the moving date, leaving the job overseas to another applicant.

Surely you can think of some similar examples instantly, either by watching other people around you or watching yourself. It is very worthwhile to look at one's own history to find examples of disguised motives and intentions.

It therefore makes sense to find a way of unlocking the basal motivation area as much as possible. Those methods suggested by Rheinberg and other scientists tend to lead back to the usage of guided fantasy journeys, i.e., imaginative pictures and fantasies, in order to unlock the impulses from the nonverbal cerebrum (and the connected parts of the limbic system).

You will find three guided fantasy journeys to explore your basal motives from page 66.

Whereas in previous editions we included these aspects briefly, we would now like to give considerably more weight to them. Therefore, from page 66 you will find three guided fantasy journeys, which you can use, if you wish, to try and find the disguised side to your motives. Do not expect to see motives and values highlighted on your mental screen. It is far more likely that you will notice moods, sensations, and emotions. Look out for your ideas and associations and continue to follow the emerging inner images, without putting any boundaries on them until you realize what the images want to tell you. Seminars and individual coaching have shown many times that fantasy journeys are an excellent preparation for the following cognitive clarification process.

Trust your system's wisdom. With a little bit of caution it will allow you to achieve coherence between the two drive systems.

You will find the section on the conscious access to your value system from page 81 onwards.

You can spend some time on developing your awareness of your motivational self-images from page 81 onwards. But in the next chapterwe first will more deeply explore the basis of self motivation – the concept of Flow.

Self-motivation begins when we can focus our ATTENTION on the pursuit of happiness, meaning, and synergy, on the spectrum of secondary drives.

It is thus important to achieve coherence between basal motives and motives we are aware of, a coherence that works. We should not try and mechanically define goals that are only apparently worth pursuing (or possibly even goals that have been projected into us to be worth pursuing by other people). Therefore, in the next chapters we will encounter the all-important question we should ask ourselves again and again: *Is it a way of the heart?*

Let us start our discovery by exploring our pursuit of happiness, an inalienable right of human beings, as stated in the American Declaration of Independence of 1776:

"The Declaration of Independence

IN CONGRESS, July 4, 1776.

The unanimous Declaration of the thirteen united States of America

... We hold these truths to be self-evident, that all men are created equal, that they are endowed by their Creator with certain unalienable Rights, that among these are Life, Liberty and the pursuit of Happiness."

Declaration of Independence: The Pursuit of Happiness

Focus 2: FLOW – The Quest For Happiness

"Most people are as happy as they want to be."
Abraham Lincoln

Aristotle wrote that *happiness* is what people want most. This means they will be especially attentive if a piece of information or an activity promises more happiness. What is it that people are looking for? What is happiness? Can we better understand what self-motivation is if we investigate the pursuit of happiness?

Aristotle
(384–322 BC) in
Nicomachean Ethics

"Why do some people love their work, have a close relationship with their family and enjoy the hours that they spend in solitary meditation, while others find their job awful, are bored at home, and are afraid of loneliness?

How can one change one's daily work routine to make it as exciting as a speedy ski race, as satisfying as singing beautiful music, as meaningful as the participation in a holy ritual?

The studies that I have performed in cooperation with other scientists indicate that such changes are possible."

Here Mihaly Csikszentmihalyi (*pronounced "Chick-sent-mee-hi"*) lists some of the central questions he has endeavored to answer during more than 30 years of research into the anatomy of human happiness, the experience of joy, and the elation associated with feeling totally connected with ourselves and the world. Most people see such experiences as a random gift of fate, but there are some who are able to integrate these experiences into their daily lives and consciously direct their energies to realizing and shaping them. The uplifting experience of having a degree of control over our own lives, of the success of an action, of gaining a deeper understanding of the matrix of factors we operate within, of being in harmony with ourselves and the world, and of taking our destiny into our own hands is what Csikszentmihalyi refers to as FLOW. He differentiates

Being in harmony
with ourselves
and the world

"True happiness,
the property
of the wise,
is stable, while
fortune's dice roll."
*Christoph Martin
Wieland*

Csikszentmihalyi:
No royal road
to FLOW

"Happiness
is a question
of awareness."

Carlos Castaneda

this particular object of his research from other forms of happiness: FLOW is a form of happiness that we can influence, in contrast to other forms of happiness, which we cannot induce deliberately (e.g., a major lotto win or meeting a dream partner).

"There is no royal road to the FLOW, and the uniqueness of each requires an individual path, but those who understand what FLOW is are able to change their lives. These changes do not depend so much on external events, but on the meaning that is given to external events. Happiness is a question of consciousness, a state for which one has to be ready, which each person has to develop and defend on his own. On rare occasions one feels elated, experiences deep joy that lasts for a prolonged time and becomes a measure for what life should be. People learn to structure their inner experiences; they can determine their quality of life. This seems to be closest to what we normally call happiness."

The ethnologist and author Carlos Castaneda reaches surprisingly similar conclusions with a completely different approach. He moved consciously away from Western science in search of a new kind of knowledge. He approached an Native Indian teacher in Mexico and, under his guidance, gained awareness and experiences that were, in some cases, rather drastic and painful.

After the especially unpleasant consequences of the consumption of the so-called *"devil's weed"*, Castaneda asked his teacher Don Juan if there would not be a way to avoid such pain. *(Happiness can here be interpreted as the deliberate and successful prevention of pain.)* Don Juan answered Castaneda's question with the following words:

". . . when I first learned about the devil's weed I realized that the plant is not right for me and I no longer pursued its path."

"Why did you decide against it, Don Juan?"

"Every time I tried the devil's weed, it nearly killed me. One time it was so bad that I thought I had reached the end. However, I could have avoided all that pain."

"Why, is there a special way to avoid pain?"

"Yes, there is a way."

"Is it a formula, a form of behavior or something else?"

"It is a way of reaching for things. When I learned about the devil's weed, I was over-eager. I reached for things in the way children reach for sweets. The devil's weed is only one of millions of ways. Each thing is only one of millions of ways ('un camino entre cantidades de caminos'). You must always remember that a way is only one of many ways. If you feel that you do not want to follow it, you must never do so. To have that much clarity requires self-discipline in your life. Only then you will know that a way is only one of many ways. And then it is not shameful for you or for others not to follow it if your heart tells you so. But your decision to stay on a way or to leave it must be free of fear or ambition. Let me warn you: Look carefully and attentively at that way. Try it as often as it seems necessary to you. Then ask yourself one, and only one question. This is a question that one asks oneself when one is old. My teacher told me the question once, when I was young and my blood was too restless to understand it. Today, I understand it. I will tell you what it is: Is this way a way of the heart? All ways are the same, because they lead nowhere. There are ways that lead through the bush or into the bush. I can say that during my life I followed long, long ways, but today I am nowhere. Today, the question of my teacher means something. Is it a way of the heart? If it is, it is a good way. If it is not, it is useless. Both ways lead nowhere, but one way is the way of the heart and the other is not. On one way the journey is full of joy, and as long as you follow it, you are one with it. The other will make you curse your life. The one makes you strong and the other weakens you."

Para mi solo recorrer los caminos que tienen corazon, cualquier camino que tenga corazon. Por ahi yo recorro, y la unica prueha que vale es atravesar todo su largo. Y por ahi yo recorro mirando, mirando, sin aliento.
Don Juan

Is it a way of the heart?

If all ways lead nowhere, does anything matter?

Is everything in vain?

How shall I then motivate myself?

How do I find my way of the heart?

Why should I follow the way of the heart?

Why not one of the many others?

Csikszentmihalyi might give us an answer. He starts his book *Finding Flow* by quoting a poem by W. H. Auden:

>*»If we really want to live,*
> *we'd better start at once to try;*
> *If we don't it doesn't matter,*
> *but we'd better start to die.«*

Csikszentmihalyi continues:

"We have a simple choice: Between now and the unavoidable end of our days we can decide to live or to die. Biologically, our life is an automatic process, as long as we maintain the necessary supplies. However, the 'life' that Auden refers to is not a process that runs automatically. In fact, everything works against that: If we do not give our life direction, it will be controlled from the outside, and will serve the interests of somebody else. Biologically programmed instincts will ensure that it expresses only what is predetermined in the genetic material. The culture will ensure that our life is used for propagating its values and institutionalized customs. Other people will try to tap as much as possible of our energy for their own interests and needs. All this happens without consideration of the effects that any of these events will have on us. We cannot expect from anyone that he will help us to live. We have to find out on our own how we want to live."

There we are again with Don Juan, who argues that it is only you yourself who alone must ask the question:

"Is it a way of the heart?"

Do not continue reading until you have answered these questions.

What makes your heart beat faster?
In which moments do you really feel happy?
What does being happy mean for you personally?

The answer is not arbitrary.

Csikszentmihalyi describes two different aspects of the process by which flow experiences are generated. One aspect relates mainly to external factors and the question of how we deal with them. It relates to our behavior and the way we psychologically experience things (see section A). The other aspect relates to the inner readiness and ability to engage in flow experiences (see section B).

A: The ten aspects of FLOW experience

A: The ten aspects of flow experience

1. FLOW experiences happen during the pursuit of self-defined goals.

The person concerned knows what he or she wants and has a clear goal.

To achieve a state of flow, we first need a task, a problem that we want to or have to solve, or a challenge that engages us. A mountaineer knows that he wants to reach the summit, a chess player wants to checkmate his opponent, and a surgeon wants to save a life.

1. Concrete Goal – a challenge

The primary goal of such people is not to become happy. They envisage something else, something very definite. Happiness is, as it were, a consequence of succeeding in the task at hand; it is an additional reward.

In our journey of discovery we will return to this phenomenon and will have a deeper insight how we can connest our with our goals. In particular, we will also see how important an exact concept of the desired goal or state is in this context.

If you imagine learning a foreign language, for example, the mere desire to learn is not sufficient to gain access to flow experiences. When can you say that you have really mastered a foreign language? In spite of all our efforts we will always find some fault, whether this involves imperfect pronunciation, doubts about grammar, or insufficient vocabulary.

It is important to know exactly what you want to attain. Do you want to be able to write an essay or a letter in Spanish? Do you want to take part in a political discussion with native Spanish speakers, or is it enough to be able to communicate in certain situations (holidays, meetings with Spanish friends, etc.)?

At this point we already want to emphasize the importance of a clear, imaginable goal. But this, of course, is not the whole story. Another central aspect – one that we will also return to in the practical exercises de- scribed later in this book – should also be noted at this early stage:

2. FLOW experiences require continuous and immediate feedback as to the degree of success of our efforts. Therefore, to be open to such experiences we need to be able to know at any given time whether we are on the right track, and how well we are doing at our task.

A chess player who is playing badly will be painfully aware that his opponent is taking more and more pieces from him. A mountaineer will be keenly aware whether he is nearing the summit or climbing the wrong way, and a surgeon sees immediately whether he is succeeding or not during an operation.

2. Immediate
feedback

To be able to determine progress in reaching a goal, feedback is required. In the case of learning Spanish, the feedback might result from being able to order a complete meal in a Spanish restaurant, without hesitation and without using a dictionary, while flirting with the waiter or waitress at the same time!

Knowledge of what we want to achieve and the success we experience on the way to our goals inspire us and intensify our concentration on our activities. We quickly notice faults, correct them, and know from new feedback that we are back on the track to success. Only on rare occasions does this feedback come from outside. In most cases, we will depend on generating it ourselves by paying close attention to what we are doing. Therefore, it is crucial that we develop evaluation criteria for our activities and learn to be aware of what is useful and what is not. In short, we need to invest energy in developing our degree of awareness. *"Happiness"*, says Csikszentmihalyi, *"depends on awareness."*

This leads us to what is possibly the most important aspect of the generation of flow experiences:

3. FLOW can only be experienced if we are actually able to handle the challenges that we create for ourselves, or to which we are exposed, on the basis of our own abilities.

FLOW experiences are generated when abilities match challenges, and when these two components exceed a certain level that we personally see as our limit. As long as we seek challenges that are proportionate to our abilities, as long as we work on the development of our abilities, and as long as we grow and learn, we will be happy. If we stop learning, we become overtaxed and frustrated. When we stop looking for new challenges, our life becomes boring.

3. Setting oneself challenging tasks proportionate to adequately developed abilities

The intermediate range in which we experience what we call happiness – the "FLOW channel" – is relatively narrow. It lies between the frustration that we experience if our expectations and goals are set too high, and the boredom and routine we experience if our abilities are not sufficiently challenged.

FLOW – a narrow span between boredom and feeling overtaxed

To stay within this "FLOW channel", it is important to have the right attitude to the tasks before us. What very few people know is that when we are confronted with a situation our brains do not merely "perceive" but also actively *"produce"* – which, in essence, means that we ourselves are able to determine how we approach a problem or a task. In principle, we can transform any activity into a FLOW experience as long as we approach it in the right way.

Every activity, of whatever kind, has the potential to generate a FLOW experience.

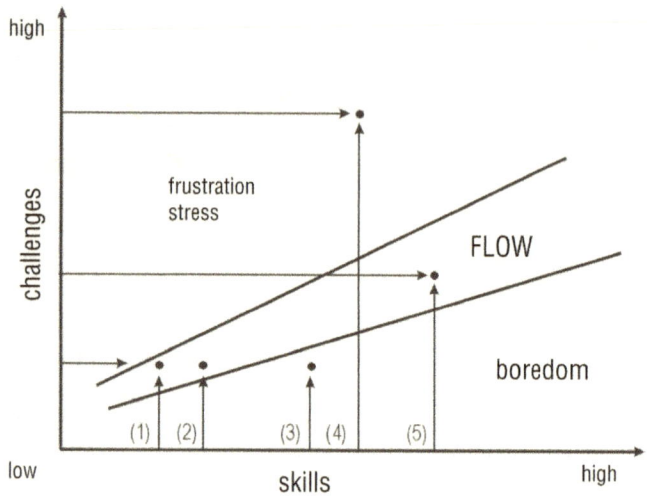

Figure 5: The FLOW channel

1. *Abilities correspond to the challenge*
2. *Repeated mastering of the same challenge – FLOW and increase in abilities – learning.*
3. *Repeated mastering of the same challenge now leads to routine – boredom due to too **few demands**.*
4. *Now, as a result of past FLOW experiences, a much greater challenge is sought out, which, in the example illustrated here, exceeds current abilities – disappointment, stress, and frustration due to **too many demands**.*
5. *A new, appropriate challenge is sought out – renewed FLOW.*

When we see an activity as a chance to generate a FLOW experience (and it is up to us whether we choose to or not), then we start to deal with our environment in a different way, i.e., we do not see it as primarily characterized by problems that are constantly hindering us. We become actively involved in shaping our own experience.

This of course requires effort on our part. If you are selecting a language course, for example, it is important to choose the right level of difficulty. Your ATTENTION has to be focused on dealing with a very specific challenge, not simply on the general idea of attending any Spanish course.

Let's take a practical example. Imagine that you have spent an extended time in a Spanish-speaking country and have made some progress in learning the language. You can order a breakfast or lunch in a restaurant, you can ask for bus connections, and after a few weeks, you manage to have a conversation about general topics such as the weather. You do not know any grammar. After returning home, you decide to learn to speak the language properly. You would surely be bored if you chose a course where the first hours were spent learning simple sentences and words that you already know. In such a situation you will not have a flow experience and you will quickly lose interest in learning Spanish. You will also not have a FLOW experience if you join a conversation class with people who are able to discuss newspaper articles that you cannot understand, because then you will be overtaxed. A language course can only be fun if you make progress in every hour, if the level of difficulty increases slowly, and if you can become aware of your abilities through practical exercises, intermediate tests, and independent, personal speaking and writing experiences.

When it comes to the chance of generating a FLOW experience, it is not so much about *what* one does as to *how* one does it.

FLOW can only occur at a level of difficulty that matches our abilities, and when we NEED ALL OUR ABILITIES to solve a problem – *when we have to struggle that little bit more and grow beyond ourselves*. FLOW occurs when we exceed our current personal limit, when we accept challenges or take a certain risk. This shows why it is not easy to experience flow in our daily work – a context in which the first two prerequisites, clear goals and immediate feedback, tend to be exceptions to the rule. In addition, many firms structure the work process to prevent faults and encourage their staff to maintain a constant level of performance – which in some cases can result in a lack of challenges.

Many people want to avoid risk and deliberately look for tasks that they can handle easily with their abilities, once they have established a match between their abilities and the type of challenges they feel they can deal with. It is characteristic of such people that they look for lots of guidance and supervision when first trying out what they feel they can manage (see next figure).

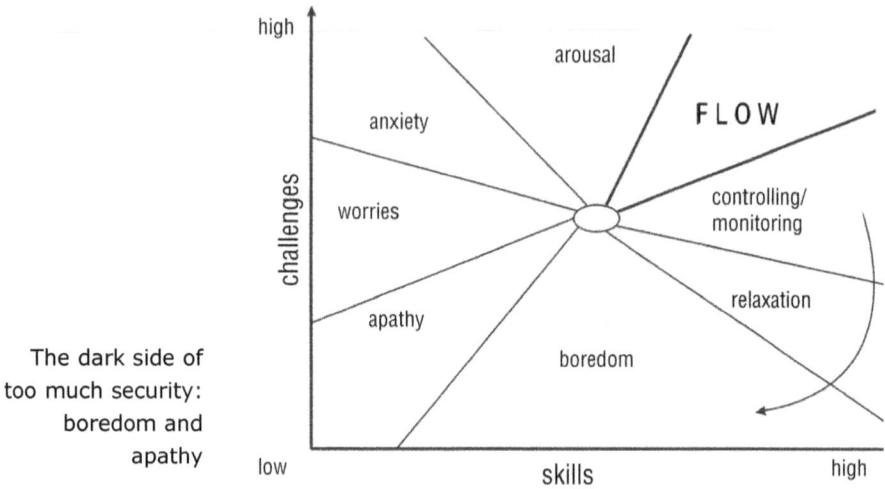

Figure 6: Emotional states outside the FLOW *channel and the dynamics of foregoing* FLOW *experiences (following Csikszentmihalyi, with reference to Massimini and Carli)*

The dark side of too much security: boredom and apathy

However, the feeling of security achieved in this way comes at a high price. It excludes the potential moments of happiness in this area that can be generated by FLOW experiences. If the refusal to handle challenges becomes a basic attitude, we might slip into a permanent state of fulfilling mere requirements, and this leads to boredom, which is only a short step away from apathy and depression. Admittedly, the two fields below the FLOW channel in Figure 6 have their positive aspects, both for the individual as well as for the organization or firm. The individual feels secure and comfortable and the firm does not risk making mistakes. However, as the Greek philosopher Heraclitus put it: *everything is in flux*. This state of affairs cannot remain stable. Gradually such a situation will develop in the direction of increasing security.

Panta rei – "everything is in flux" *Heraclitus*

Given a constant level of challenge, tasks will be handled better and better, with the result that abilities in this area will constantly improve. In the end, these tasks will cease to demand a high level of concentration. We will not feel personally involved anymore and we will increasingly lose the feeling that our actions have any significance. Once we have reached this point, FLOW experiences become only a distant potential, and given that many people experience their working life in this way, it is hardly surprising that more and more of them are looking for stimulation and FLOW experiences in their leisure time.

It is important to emphasize here that we are talking about a trend, not an steadfast rule. Research carried out by Csikszentmihalyi and his colleagues in various countries indicate that the majority of people continue to gain the majority of experiences of happiness from their work and not from their leisure time. We might dream of a work-free weekend and holidays, and temporary laziness can be good for us and help us to regenerate and gain new energy. However, we will still tend to find more happiness in activity, in meeting challenges, in increasing our competence and extending our limits. A well-structured work environment and good leadership should ensure that, in addition to those areas that require faultless work, every staff member is faced with an *additional* field of tasks in which he or she can take risks, meet challenges, and experience personal growth.

> Most people experience happiness more frequently during their work than during their leisure time.

This leads us directly to the fourth aspect of flow experiences.

4. FLOW experiences are associated with the feeling that success is – at least in principle – a result of our own efforts, the feeling that it is possible to guide and monitor how we deal with tasks even though the actual outcome of our efforts is not yet clear.

To reach the state of FLOW we need to have the confidence that we can influence our situation at least to a certain degree, that we can guide the process we are involved in, or have control over the way we achieve results. When we learn, we become better at what we do. As a result, we become better at avoiding many of the mistakes we made initially. We gain more control over the process we are engaged in, and we become better at recognizing which steps we have to take next.

> 4. The task seems, in principle, to be solvable – although the outcome remains unknown.

On the other hand, it is important that our abilities do not reach a level where the chance of failure is completely excluded. A chess game with an inferior opponent that is over in ten minutes does not generate a FLOW experience. One of the preconditions for experiencing FLOW is thus that the challenge we are facing lies near the very limit of our current possibilities.

Let us now consider the side effects, consequences, and deeper meaning of this kind of experience of happiness.

5. Intense concentration focuses our ATTENTION on a limited field of stimuli and information. Other problems and worries in our daily lives are excluded.

5. Intense concentration

Everyday concerns fade into the background

In the case of a FLOW experience, intense concentration on the essential aspects of our task or situation result in us ignoring hunger, thirst, and other distractions for as long as we are involved in the process. Stimuli that are not directly related to dealing with the task at hand are not consciously registered.

Take the example of a chess game. As long as we are concentrating on the pieces or considering which moves the opponent has in mind, we easily forget that we have been bending over the board for three hours and that we have actually been a little hungry from the start of the game …

6. The limits of the ego seem to disappear, consciousness and action merge, and there are moments when we become oblivious to our surroundings.

6. Forgetting the self

We experience a feeling of lightness, of flowing or floating. We become absorbed in our activity and our own ego loses its importance. (This *"activity"* does not necessarily have to be "active;" it might also entail "passively," yet attentively, listening to music, watching a theatre play, watching a sports game or reading a good book.)

7. The sense of time is lost or altered.

7. Altered sense of time

Sometimes time seems to stand still, sometimes the moments drag endlessly, and sometimes time seems to "fly." (*It seems that in such moments the dominance of the verbal hemisphere of the cerebrum, which is also responsible for the chronological, linear perception of time, is at least temporarily suspended, while the other, non-verbal hemisphere becomes more activated.)*

8. The experience becomes autotelic, i.e., it becomes a goal in itself (auto: self, telos: goal).

The desired result is the successful completion of the action, the realization of a self-defined goal. (In the above passive examples a deeper understanding, recognition of the idea of the artist, or an understanding of complex interconnections may serve the same purpose.) Hopes and speculations concerning external rewards or recognition have a lesser importance (which does not mean they have no importance). FLOW experiences can thus occur when the motivation for an activity comes from within us. They do not occur when the activity is triggered merely by the prospect of a reward (e.g., in the form of a bonus or a promotion), or when the goals are set by others and we cannot identify with them.

> 8. The success of the action is more important than the prospect of external rewards.

It is easy to do things that are fun. For example, improvising on a musical instrument is enjoyable in itself, while at the same time it brings us closer to our goal of one day playing with other musicians in a group.

To experience FLOW, it should be the enjoyment of the activity that motivates you and not the fact that it could bring an external reward on completion. It can obviously be gratifying and satisfactory to be rewarded for a performance, whether this is in the form of praise from a superior or a salary increase. But let us be honest: Did the possibility of praise make the process any easier or more pleasant? Did it make the long process more pleasant or generate a FLOW experience?

It may very well be that we dislike a task at the outset but become enthusiastic about it after working on it for some time. However, in order to generate a FLOW experience from our work the motivation for our efforts must come from within us.

> From extrinsic to intrinsic motivation

9. Successfully dealing with a challenge is rewarded by an increase in the complexity of one's personality.

Complexity is the simultaneous and synergetic increase of:

Greater
competence
through more
complexity:
the delicate
interplay between
acquiring
and creating
understanding

* **Differentiation** (increase of knowledge, individualization, specialization)

* **Integration** (understanding the interconnections, interactions, and networks linking the elements acquired through differentiation to the whole system and to other people, institutions, and ideas)

Csikszentmihalyi sees the increase of complexity as a successful combination of two contradictory tendencies and forces.

Countering
the danger of
egocentrism
without sinking
into conformity

"Differentiation means a move towards uniqueness, towards separation of the self from others. Integration means the opposite: Connection with other people, thoughts and structures beyond the self. A complex personality is one that manages to combine these two contradictory tendencies. A self that is only differentiated but not integrated may achieve great individual results, but it is at risk of getting caught in egocentric thinking. A person whose self is exclusively based on integration lives connected and safe, but he lacks independent individuality. Only if psychological energy is diverted into both processes, and selfishness as well as conformity are avoided, can the self achieve true complexity."

"I do not disdain
knowledge . . . (but
what we must do)
is learn how to
learn, whet our
appetites for know-
ledge in order to be
able to enjoy per-
forming a task, to
feel the excitement
of creativity, to
learn to love what
we are doing and
to find what we
would like to do."
*Albert Szent-
Györgyi*

There is a dangerous tendency to think that all internal processes should be (and can be) speeded up. And indeed, the last three decades have seen a dramatic acceleration in the increase and communication of knowledge – i.e., differentiation – that has been driven by technology and a spirit of invention in the external world. However, when it comes to the internal process of integration, networking ideas and information, understanding interconnections, and establishing or changing structures in the course of processing information in our brains, technology does not help us. Without an increase in understanding, the one-sided increase in knowledge leads not to increased complexity but increased *complicatedness*, to an increase in what Csikszentmihalyi calls "psychic entropy," or simply to mental and emotional confusion – i.e., to the exact opposite of the desired state of happiness. Lothar Seiwert – who has written a number of books vividly documenting his own development from a time-management trainer to a trainer in the "art of living" – points out that if we are looking for a better under-standing of ourselves, others, and the way the world works, we urgently require a *deceleration*, a *"discovery of slowness."*

10. The increase of complexity leads to growth of the self.

Psychic entropy (an inner confusion that is experienced as a feeling of pressure or tension) is reduced through the success of an activity, by reaching a self-defined goal within a structured field.

10. Personal growth: greater competence, greater flexibility, inner peace

The reduction of tension and the deep sense of joy and relaxation that follows are described as a flowing, liber-ating, floating feeling of lightness, as a feeling of ela-tion. We experience harmony, or as Hansch would call it, synergy. Body and mind are in harmony with each other and with the world, i.e., in FLOW. These are the moments we feel in close contact with our purpose in life.

Csikszentmihalyi's research has led him to the conclu-sion that people who attain a state of FLOW use less mental energy than people who have to struggle to con-centrate because they are bored or afraid. He regards the state of FLOW as just as intrinsic to human beings as the information-processing function of the brain. In his view the fun of learning is as natural as the pleasure of sexuality, and both support the evolutionary goals of humans, i.e., the preservation of their species.

FLOW activities require less mental energy than negative states such as fear and boredom – and they are intrinsic to human nature.

Games, artistic activities, purposeful work, and reli-gious rituals are good examples of such FLOW-oriented activities. But practically any activity can generate an optimal or FLOW experience, as long as the above mentioned criteria are fulfilled. This then constitutes one side of the coin: ten aspects relating to external factors, how we deal with them, and the nature of the associated psychological experiences.

We now turn to the other side: our inner readiness and ability to open ourselves to FLOW experiences.

B: The inner readiness for FLOW experiences

B. The inner preparedness for FLOW experiences

The second set of conditions concerns our inner attitude. Some people have an exceptional talent for adapting their abilities to the externally available possibilities. They set themselves reachable goals, even if in situations where it seems there is actually nothing for them to do. They can see feedback where others see nothing. They can concentrate easily and are difficult to distract. Because they have no fear of losing touch with themselves, they have no trouble forgetting about themselves where required.

People who have learned to direct their awareness in this way have a "FLOW personality." They do not have to be playing a game to experience FLOW. They can be happy working on an assembly line or even sitting in solitary confinement.

We certainly do not want to pre-empt the scientists engaged in the study of the potential role played in this context by genetic factors and upbringing, and to what extent development and learning independent of these background factors is possible. All this needs further research. However, it is at least worth noting here that Bertrand Russell, one of the greatest philosophers of the 20th century, described his own path to happiness as a learning process: *"I learned slowly to become indifferent towards myself and my shortcomings. I concentrated my attention more and more on external objects: the state of the world, the different areas of knowledge, individuals whom I liked."* Csikszentmihalyi is convinced that the ability to be happy *"lends itself to development, and is an ability that can be perfected through training and discipline."*

And, as we recall, Castaneda offers us the observation: *"To have that much clarity, you need self-discipline in your life."* Even the ancient Romans had the proverb *per aspera as astra,* meaning the way to the stars is paved with effort and difficulty.

If we accept that we have to invest in our future happiness, that happiness does not fall from the sky but is something that we experience again and again as the result of our own efforts, that stimulating self-motivation is a process to which we have to dedicate all our attention, then we should consider precisely what kind of activities we want to engage in to generate FLOW experiences.

In his book *FLOW – the Secret of Happiness* Csikszent-mihalyi describes people who live a relatively happy and satisfied life due to their ability to generate as much flow as possible in their work and their relationships. However, he points out that it is difficult to lead a happy life solely on the basis of the serial generation of flow experiences.

From the individual "kick" to the discovery of a theme for life

In this case, the whole is more than the sum of its parts. An artist might paint for years and enjoy every minute of it, but then become depressed and dispirited when he grows older and his ideas repeat themselves, and when he has to wait longer for the next creative impulse. A professional tennis player who has lived for his career might, nevertheless, end up as a disappointed and bitter person if he is not able to find a different flow channel in another area of life once his career is over. The belief in a value system that gives purpose and direction to our personal lives makes it easier to convert the whole of our lives into a harmonic FLOW experience. FLOW can only become a guideline on how to lead one's life if it is linked to what one considers meaningful.

A system of values that gives life meaning and direction

The key to lifelong experiences of happiness is not the pursuit of flow as an intensely stimulating experience, but to consider carefully in which areas of life you would like to experience FLOW. If it is possible to generate

FLOW experiences that coincide with the realization of values, of personal ideals, then the chance of repeatedly experiencing FLOW in the long term is much higher than if our focus is merely on achieving the next "kick."

If we apply this concept to the professional area, particularly to the context of leadership, then it follows that managers and staff members need to be able to recognize and define meaning in their activities in connection with the principles and goals of the company. They have to ask themselves what is really important and essential for them. They have to achieve clarity about overlaps between the goals of the company and their own goals and where conflicts or tensions might occur.

These aspects of values and meaning, which Victor Frankel and Walter Böckmann, in particular, have emphasized, will be dealt with in more detail in the next chapter.

FLOW experiences are not simply given to us. The extension of our abilities is often preceded by a longer phase of frustration. To reach self-defined growth targets it is necessary to learn new things. As the next figure shows, understanding only increases continually in parallel to what is learned for a short period. After some time, one reaches a phase where no more improvement takes place. This is called a "plateau phase." It is connected with a loss of self-motivation due to the person no longer seeing any progress and perhaps even feeling too stupid to solve the task at hand. Doubt and fear set in.

"The common denominator of all successful people is endurance."
Napoleon Hill

If one does not quit during this phase and instead continues or makes even more of an effort, what has previously been incomprehensible will suddenly become clear and self-doubt will evaporate. Growth means learning, and because our brain works in a way that is based on this kind of "leap" between plateaus, experiencing growth involves accepting the interplay between longer phases of frustration and short experiences of success.

Our brains need time to establish new links. Therefore, when you find yourself in a situation where you feel unable to psychologically absorb anything, it is important to not to abandon the task at hand, while at the same time allowing yourself to take breaks.

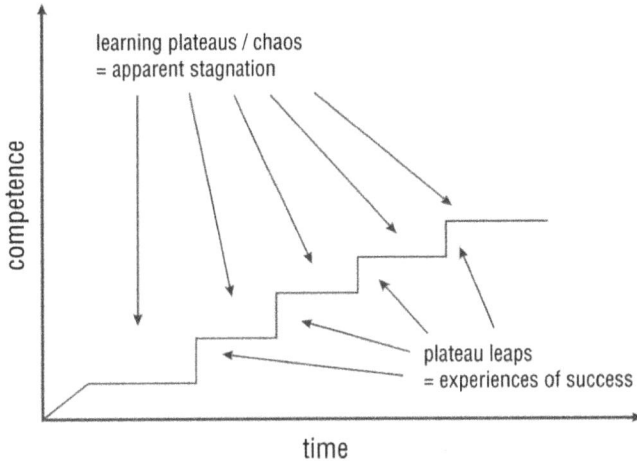

Learning that human growth, achieving goals, proceeds via long plateau phases, which involve stagnation and frustration.

Figure 7: Plateaus – levels in the learning process

During the plateau phase you will not notice any progress, although your brain will continue working in the background and form new frameworks of understanding. It is even possible to do other things during such phases, as long as you "keep your eye on the ball."

After some time, the next leap in learning will occur. However, if you feel that you are not progressing at all, it is often helpful simply to sleep on the task or problem you are dealing with. You will usually find that *"enlightenment"* comes to you quite naturally the following day.

What you should definitely try not to do is panic! This generates stress, which causes synaptic blockage and prevents the brain from functioning properly. If you do experience panic, you should stop trying to learn immediately and use your preferred method of deep relaxation.

It is important to enjoy intermediate successes and to really celebrate them!

Think
of the farmer who
did not think of
tugging at his
wheat so that it
might grow faster.

Each leap between plateaus makes a new flow experience possible and generates a form of motivation that grows from within (so-called intrinsic motivation), and is far more powerful and durable than any promise of external reward (*extrinsic* motivation). But do not overtax yourself! And do not expect intrinsic motivation to simply be there from the beginning. Intrinsic motivation can only develop after a certain period of time. We first need to develop our abilities to a level that enables us to deal with challenges that are demanding enough to facilitate a flow experience. Figures 7 and 8 clearly illustrate the interdependency of these two aspects.

The secret of
self-motivation:
making the leap
from extrinsic to
intrinsic motivation

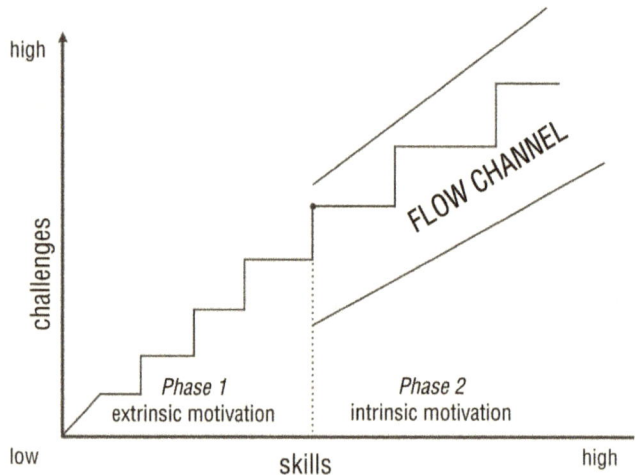

Figure 8: Two phases of motivation (extrinsic and intrinsic) in the flow model

Treat yourself
to something you
really enjoy –
and then, at the
right time, allow
your intrinsic
motivation to
provide you with
a much more
intensive feeling
of happiness (see
reward list p. 262).

It is, therefore, a good idea on the first leg of your "learning journey" (which we recommend you divide up using four or five intermediate goals) to provide yourself with attractive extrinsic rewards (you can find initial ideas in Appendix 2, from page 262). However, once you have first experienced FLOW in this particular area, it is vital that you "switch" to intrinsic motivation and aim for the next FLOW experience. Continuing to rely on external reward will undermine the whole process and it will not function in the longer term. A good FLOW experience has to be properly prepared. We recommend proceeding in four steps.

In the first step it is helpful to remember previous FLOW experiences you may have had. These do not necessarily have to be "peak" experiences. FLOW experiences are also possible in the routine of daily life. Here, Csikszentmihalyi offers a characterization that can help ensure that you select a real FLOW experience, one that you can distinguish from other pleasant experiences.

Have you looked at the wide range of possible rewards in the appendix?

"In the state of FLOW, action follows action according to an inherent logic that does not seem to require conscious intervention by the person performing the actions. He experiences the process as a continuous flow from one moment to the next; he feels that he is the master of the process, that there is hardly a separation between him and the environment, between stimulus (external signals and impulses) and reaction or between past, present and future."

In the second step you should consider the array of possible challenges. Do you want to have a FLOW experience in the professional area, with your partner, with your family, do you want to be the winner of a game, achieve a triumph in sports, or understand something that has previously seemed too complicated and inaccessible?

In the third step you should select one of these possibilities and focus your energies on it. If you want a flow experience that is not based "merely" on the momentary sensation of happiness, but is enhanced by a feeling of purpose and meaning, then you should first work through the next chapter before choosing your challenge. In this chapter we will deal in detail with the connection between the experience of happiness and the implementation of values.

(Once you have made your decision, you can proceed to the fourth step, which involves a detailed description of the challenge you have selected. If you continue to accompany us on this journey, you will notice more and more that your level of ATTENTION at different moments in your life has increased, and that you can focus your ATTENTION more sharply. This enables you to "bundle" your energy and enhances your motivation.)

STOP

**www.
mypurpose.de**

"There is no-one
who has achieved
something ordinary
without wanting to
achieve something
extraordinary."
*Marie von Ebner-
Eschenbach*

Set up the conditions for generating your first conscious flow experience now!

- Think of a personal FLOW experience (or several of them) and describe the feeling of happiness you had.

- Think of how this FLOW experience was generated.

- Select your next personal challenge: first list all your present possibilities of having a FLOW experience.

- Selection – now answer the question: Which challenge do I want to take on next?

And then:

- What do I need to learn? What resources do I still not have?

- For the moment, just keep a hold of these ideas. You should take further concrete steps only after working through the fourth chapter. Before proceeding, we need to work more on the question of appropriate challenges and the necessity of the precise formulation of these challenges.

Once you've got to this point, you should think of a few types of extrinsic motivation that particularly appeal to you. You can find some ideas in the appendix 2, page 262 ff.

With regard to very simple goals concerning our everyday life, or if you already have sufficient inner motivation, you may refrain from deriving the goals from the value system initially, in order to save time. Go straight to Chapter 4, p. 103ff (The Goal Scenario). Should you notice when conducting your plan that you are running lower and lower on motivation, we strongly advise you to return to this part of the book and to continue on the following page.

If you decide to read Chapter 3 later and want to engage in writing down your goals immediately, continue with Chapter 4 on page 103.

The following third chapter is intended for those readers who are keen to explore their most important and meaningful life goals.

Focus 3: Values – recognizing the forces that drive us

"We do not need new values, we need the courage to live according to those we have." Gundl Kutschera

Preliminary note:

We would like to provide a further practical hint here. This is a book that encourages you to engage intensively with yourself. However, it is extremely useful when engaged in a process of "self-experience" to also consciously direct your ATTENTION to other people. Above all, you may find it helpful to take a closer look at the people who have a positive effect on you, people who could provide you with a role model. It is important to realize that the strongest form of extrinsic motivation comes from people whom we encounter regularly in our daily environment. Do you consciously select the people with whom you maintain contact? Are they people who inspire you and who open up new perspectives for you? *How much do these people influence your value system and in what way do you influence your fellow human beings? Can you picture yourself being a role model?*

In the last chapter we saw that it is not just any activity that can provide us with the experience of happiness, of FLOW. It is only when the things we engage in have meaning that individual experiences of happiness can lead to a happy life in the long term.

The challenges that we seek have to be related to a sense of purpose that runs through our lives. Otherwise our successes will have a stale aftertaste, in spite of the momentary elation we experience when we achieve something.

In this context it is useful to look at the work of Viktor Frankl, who argues that the traditional psychoanalytical understanding of human beings was too limited. Frankl also rejects behaviorism and Gestalt psychology as insufficient explanatory models, since they tend to see people as purely determined by drives or the maintenance of physiological/biological homeostasis (i.e., the attempt to maintain equilibrium). While it is true that the way human beings function does involve homeostatic "feedback loops," this does not mean that the human being represents a system in equilibrium. Rather, people who are consciously aware of themselves seek to build up "creative tensions." Moreover, "people are not free of limitations, but that does not make them limited people; they have the freedom to take a stance ... People have drives but they are not driven beings; they make something of their drives, but they are not made of them."

Frankl argues that people have a *"will to meaning"* and the possibility of *"achieving meaning by implementing values."* The *"authority"* ruling decision-making, the conscience, is an inherent part of the individual and determines which *"value"* he or she has to implement in a certain situation. Meaning, as Frankl understands it, is an individual as well as a situational valuation that has to be decided and implemented anew at every moment of life.

What are our values? How do we find out which of the value systems anchored deep within us determines the decisions we make?

Frankl discriminates between three value categories:

- Creative values (doing, shaping, creating, realizing the possibilities inherent in people relating to externally oriented or externally recognizable work)

- Experiential (social) values (the area of social perception, encounters with other people)

- Attitudinal values (the possibility of experiencing meaning in our attitude in relation to situations we cannot alter, dealing with such situations, the ability

to realize creative or experiential values while growing beyond or transcending our own limitations)

What is important to a person or what is valuable has
meaning. Regarding something as valuable means
giving the thing, state, task, or person importance, relevance, i.e., value.

Values determine where we direct our ATTENTION, and
they have a decisive influence on our behavior. The
key to a balanced and happy life is to live our own life
according to the highest ideals. We have to act continuously in accordance with the principles we think
our lives are about. But we can only do this once we
are aware what our values actually are. The values by
which we orient our lives are the signposts that give
our lives direction. These values are the cause of decisions we make to do certain things and not to do
others. And it is the sum of all these decisions that
determines the direction our lives take; it is from these
decisions that the essential themes or fundamental
ideas that guide our lives grow.

It is when we do not feel there is meaning in what we
do that we become aware of a "value deficit," and this
drives us to seek out the values that are important to
us. The reason for many frustrations, disappointments,
feeling of lack of fulfillment, and the nagging suspi-
cion that one's whole life could be completely different, results, to a large extent, from the fact that people
are focused on instant gratification rather than the pro-
found sense of happiness that results from the fulfillment of values. An astounding number of people give
up on living according to a system of values. This is
often due to a lack of clarity about their own value system, to the fact that several contradictory values are
pursued at the same time, and to the common tendency to pursue values for a time and then to *"forget"*
about them, once a partying teenager turns into a focused and successful manager.

> A lack of clarity regarding one's own value system is the source of much frustration.

And yet a tremendous power can be derived from
living in accordance with a value orientation. Being in

The source of energy, strengths, and inner stability is congruence. Congruence means living in accordance with one's own positive values

– and we have a warning system that lets us know when we are not living in congruence with our value system.

congruence, in accord with meaningful principles, generates a feeling of inner security, an external air of certainty, and determination, and the kind of inner calm and serenity that most people ultimately aspire to.

Csikszentmihalyi points out the problems that can develop if we only look for FLOW experiences in areas that can provide us with an immediate "kick." The problem here is that the human "system" is fundamentally orientated to the *realization of values*. If we do not orient our behavior towards the realization of values over the longer term, our organism reacts not only by failing to produce experiences of happiness, but by generating pain, uneasiness, inner tension, and feelings of pressure. It seems that we are equipped with a protective mechanism designed to ensure that we live according to our value system.

Unfortunately, we tend to handle this intelligent and sensitive protective system in a very unintelligent way. When faced with the kind of negative effects described above we tend not to change our behavior in a way that better corresponds to our value system.

On the contrary, we combat such pain by quickly "intervening" in our brain's biochemistry to alter the hormonal processes that are in fact warning us something is wrong. Our aim here is to replace the pain we are experiencing with – at the least – a state of indifference or even a short-term, manufactured sense of happiness. What this means in concrete terms is that we smoke, drink alcohol, eat too much, engage obsessively in loveless sex, abuse drugs, attempt to dominate others – perhaps even violently, spend hours watching TV and playing computer games, or try to lose ourselves in work.

But what is the real problem here?

These behavior patterns are indeed the result of the kind of frustration, anger, and inner emptiness felt by people who do not experience their lives as meaningful.

They try to get rid of these unpleasant feelings by doing something that promises a quick change in their emotional state. Such behavior quickly turns into a pattern. However, because these behavior patterns do not make people happy, they subsequently find themselves trying to change them.

Anthony Robbins addresses this problem in his book *The Robbins Power Principle*. While people are always searching for ways to stop drinking alcohol, to eat less, and to stop smoking, in most cases they do not confront the underlying reasons for their problem.

According to Robbins, the issue is not that somebody has an alcohol problem, but that he or she has a value problem. The only reason why people drink is because they feel a need to change an emotional state that they otherwise cannot bear. Their internal alarm system is intact and warns them that something is wrong by means of pain, inner pressure, and discomfort. However, they have found ways to stabilize their internal state, to restore a feeling of well-being.

Addiction problems are primarily value problems.

The problem is that the "anesthetic" substances involved have to be taken at ever-shorter intervals and in ever-increasing amounts (because our primary biological system adapts to them) to cope with the inner tension that repeatedly builds up. As a result, people spend a lot of time, energy, and money trying to free themselves from their own methods of numbing themselves emotionally. However, they are approaching the problem from the wrong perspective. Their real problem is that they are not aware of what is actually important in their lives.

In the long term, the attempt to combat dependencies has less and less effect if we do not deal with the root cause of the underlying tensions.

The change that occurs when a person lives up to his or her own standards, when they see their values fulfilled and live according to them, results in an intense feeling of happiness.

People who live and act in accordance with their inner orientation have a strong sense of this harmony, this congruence. These people develop a feeling of self-esteem, inner stability, and strength, and **their ATTEN-TION is not focused on avoiding or reducing pain but on realizing values.** They do not allow themselves to be manipulated and they have a clear concept of what constitutes a *"welcome new experience."*

The creation of a "cognitive dissonance"

If somebody decides that from January 1 onwards, they will not smoke, then they have accepted the value of being a non-smoker into their value system.

January 1 comes around and the person manages not to smoke. The value they have accepted and their actual behavior now correspond. They experience a feeling of inner strength and a consistent level of self-esteem (see Figure 9a).

On January 4, the person starts working. Their secretary has sent a fax from her holiday resort, stating that she has a broken shin and will stay off work for another week. When they start up their computer the hard drive crashes. Then their boss asks for important documents that they need at 11:00 a.m. because they have to go to a conference in Brussels. Our model person gets into a panic. To calm down and find the documents they light up their first cigarette (see Figure 9b).

There is already some discrepancy between value and real behavior, but at first they smoke only one cigarette. Then things get worse. During the conference in Brussels it is decided that a part of the company will be transferred to London. Now our model person not only finds that they have a great deal of work pressure but that they must also worry about their own future position. Our subject's secretary then decides to take the remainder of her annual leave and stay at the holiday resort in the care of the resident doctor. After one week our non-smoker is again smoking their usual quota – in the interest of the company, of course. They have to keep a cool head and know that they are much better at doing this if they have another cigarette (see Figure 9c).

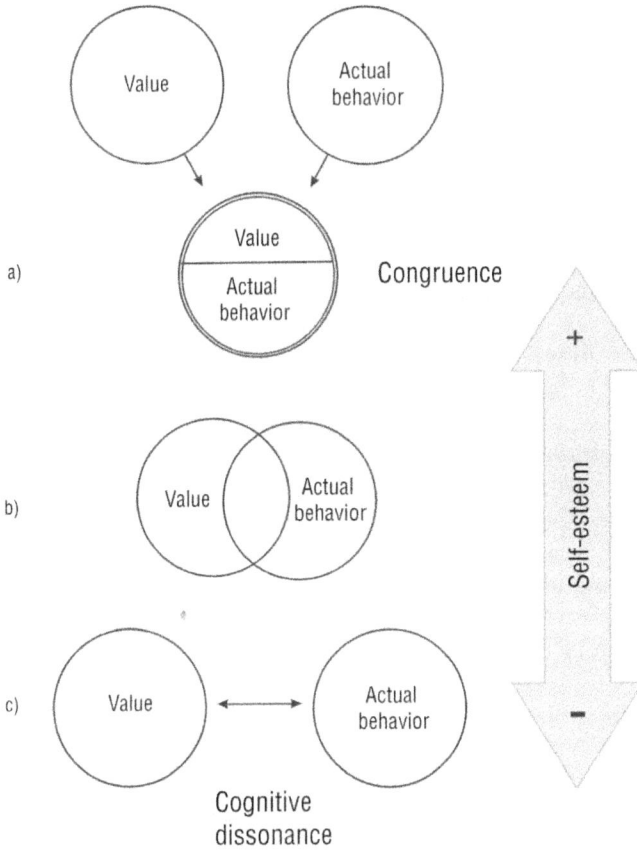

Figure 9 a/b/c: When value and actual behavior correspond, self-esteem is high. When behavior deviates from the value system, self-esteem decreases.

Now value and actual behavior do not correspond at all. The result is a *"cognitive dissonance."* Our model person knows that something is wrong, and the result is an extremely unpleasant feeling of tension in the stomach and the heart. This feeling constitutes a neural alarm. Our organism is requesting action!

Our internal alarm indicates something is wrong with our "system."

There are three ways of handling cognitive dissonance:

1. The person concerned changes his value (e.g., accepts he is a smoker)

2. The person changes his actual behavior (e.g., does not smoke anymore, whatever happens around him)

3. The person finds a good reason/excuse *(e.g., why he cannot possibly stop smoking completely right now)*

Everything gets more expensive; only the excuses get cheaper.
Popular saying

You may guess which option most people choose. Correct! They find a good excuse.

"It is precisely the inconsequential things in life that have the greatest consequence."
André Gide

Freud wrote that people are not rational but rationalizing beings. And "rationalization" is precisely what we do when we find excuses for doing something that contradicts our value system. Yet when we persist in doing this, and possibly even use various "anesthetic" substances to dull the sense of dissonance, this can lead to massive inner tension, stress-induced damage to our immune system, and even serious psychosomatic illnesses. Our self-esteem is ruined and our attention is increasingly focused on finding the next *"anesthetic."*

The experience of tension is a consequence rather than a cause.

Once this cycle is established it is not easy to break, and it is, therefore, important to prevent it getting started in the first place. We need to find out what gives us a sense of meaning and live our lives accordingly. Luckily, the decision to start this project can be made at any time, and we would like to encourage especially those who might feel they have been slipping into a state of dissonance for some time.

Seeking challenges that enable us to realize our values.

At this point, we need to extend Csikszentmihalyi's two-dimensional flow model with a third dimension and combine the pursuit of challenges with the dimension of our personal values. Once we stop merely looking for challenges that provide a "kick" and instead focus on challenges in areas that also involve realizing our own values, then the experience of FLOW is combined with an experience of value and thus gains a lasting quality of purpose and meaning. Hansch has shown that experiences in the secondary motivational area (i.e., the search for happiness, meaning, and transcendence) tend to endure because they open a range of developmental and learning processes.

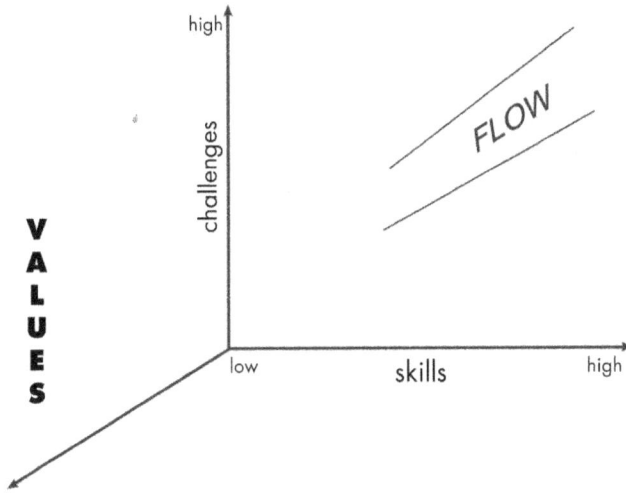

A decisive step:

Adding a third dimension to the FLOW model by linking FLOW experiences with our personal value systems

Figure 10: The third dimension of the flow model – deriving challenges from values

As Covey points out, we require a big and powerful "YES" to be able to say the many little "nos" to the temptations of our primary system, of our baser instincts, as well as the occasional "no" to demands made on us by other people and institutions. In this chapter we want to focus our ATTENTION on discovering this big "YES".

In order to be able to resist the temptations of our *baser instincts*, we require a big YES – a clarity about what is important to us.

At this point you can already begin to prepare for the practical exercises we will outline later.

• Identify the values that are important for you in various areas of your life

• Sort these values by importance

• Focus on the values you would most like to realize

• Consider what these values mean to you

Regularly working on one's values, adding new values, and discarding values that are no longer important can lead to "self-reinvention."

The possibility of reinventing ourselves

> *Being able to identify or redefine one's own values is a particularly important step toward self-motivation. Carrying out this process means you having reached the decisive turning point that enables you to increasingly protect yourself from manipulation by others and your environment and to live your own life.*

CAUTION:
Do not
underestimate
the importance
of basal motives!
(see page 27
onwards)

CAUTION: As much as we may stress the importance of engaging consciously with our own values, we should not forget the meaning of that part of the human drive system that we are *not* aware of. We have already stressed this point very specifically at the beginning (see page 27 onwards). Referring to, among others, D.C. McClelland, Rheinberg points out the importance of the so-called **basal motives**, which we are not easily conscious of. They are different to the **motivational self-images**, which we know already or are at least able to recognize relatively easily. Only if there is no contradiction between basal and cognitive values are we able to truly answer the question: *"Is it a way of the heart?"* with a "Yes."

Hence we will only then look at the conscious parts of our motivational structures (from page 81 onwards) when we have first dealt in detail with the basal drives. (If you would like to skip the respective fantasy journey exercises at first – continue on page 81 with the text.)

A.
The basal motives

A. Tracking the motives: Do you sense your basal motives?

The preparation of guided fantasy journeys

The preparation
of guided
fantasy journeys

Shared fantasies have proven to be an insightful procedure to track one's basal drives. If you haven't experienced such fantasy journeys yet please read the following introduction first and follow the preparation exercise (page 69). Otherwise, start immediately on page 73.

Introduction and preparation of shared fantasies

These exercises are based on many years of experience and they have proven to be safe and extremely effective, even when first impressions are sometimes only weak and faint. Shared fantasy journeys, however, do not pursue therapeutic goals and should not be conducted by people who are currently emotionally overstrained without being accompanied by a professional. People who are, or have been, receiving psychotherapy should consider doing this exercise together with their therapist.

If you find that the exercises give rise to strong, negative emotions, you should stop the exercise, count backwards from ten to one, then open your eyes and do some physical exercises in order to achieve a completely conscious state again.

Should strong and negative emotions develop, we recommend stopping the exercise by counting backwards from ten to one, opening your eyes, and doing some physical exercises in order to become fully awake again.

You can either create a recording of the text yourself – please do not forget to leave long enough pauses in between the individual image proposals – or ask somebody else in who's proximity you feel good and comfortable to read the various texts very slowly to you, with the respective pauses of approximately 30 seconds. Please use a watch, as our sense of time can sometimes be very misleading.

Before you begin, make sure you have a pen and adequate paper ready.

---

a.) Introduction:
   Two types of internal seeing

There are two types of internal seeing, which can be engaged separately from one another or linked together.

Introduction into training the power of the imagination

One type of visualization consists in the revival of memories. With our inner eye we see what we, at some point, have actually seen and experienced in our lives. We can describe this as calling up saved images.

The second type of visualization consists in the construction of an imagined image. Using the creative power of our own imagination we create a completely new image. We imagine something in a form that we have not actually experienced. This second way of seeing is more demanding than the first. And, as adults, we often find it rather strange.

Many people will be familiar with this type of non-realistic seeing from their schooldays: "Stop dreaming and do your homework." We are accustomed to prohibitions on this type of imaginative wandering, and it often takes some time before we become accustomed to it being possible again.

Give yourself permission now!

And have patience with yourself. If you are not used to working with mental images, be aware that it will take some time until your imagination achieves the kind of power it needs to produce something new.

The following exercises allow the real, the remembered, and the freely imagined to be blended together. Given that you allow yourself the necessary time, this is the best way to discover your own unique imagination. Do not put yourself under pressure. Allow the images to come of their own accord. Do not try to create them. However, deliberately creating them is not necessarily a problem. It can even help to increase your own imaginative powers. Sometimes it is not images that emerge but feelings, noises, and scents. Simply register everything as it happens. Refrain from judging or assessing. If you find you cannot relax, do a few strenuous physical exercises. Or dance to whatever your favorite music is at the moment. You will find that this kind of physical exertion will leave you calmer and more able to turn inwards.

The imagination training is followed by two fantasy journeys, which may provide you with an indication as to the direction in which your "genius" would like to move, to unfold. When exploring the imagination, the best approach is to remain calm but also playful and curious. Allow yourself to be surprised and, above all, leave yourself enough time for interpretation and conclusions.

When experiencing guided fantasy journeys it is most effective to adopt both a playful serenity and a childlike curiosity. Just let yourself be surprised and, above all, leave yourself enough time for associations and interpretations.

b.) Preparation:
To be able to relax

(Readers who are experienced in doing guided fantasies can start immediately with the first guided fantasy journey on page 73.)

First of all, make sure that anything that could potentially disturb you is eliminated. Thus take a room that is available for you entirely (put up a sign stating: Please do not disturb!). Switch off telephones, music, TV, etc.

In order to become immersed in the world of fantasy journeys, it is helpful to try and consciously relax beforehand using some kind of relaxation method.

Important: Learn how to consciously relax!

Autogenic training, progressive muscle relaxation by Jacobsen, yoga, biofeedback – certain forms of meditation are established techniques to place one into a comfortable state of inner calm.

Many people experience a comfortable state of relaxation after having been to sauna or after playing intensive sport. Choose what suits you and what is within easy reach for you.

If you are not able to relax, do some physical exercises first and really push yourself. Or dance to your favorite music. This will enable you to look inside yourself with more inner calm.

If you don't know any relaxation techniques do the following: Lie flat on your back on the floor with your legs parallel and arms next to your torso. It is important to leave your hands straight and relaxed and not in a fist. Lay your head comfortably onto a pillow. Alternatively, you can sit yourself in a very comfortable armchair. Now close your eyes and prepare for the inner images. Breathe in deeply and let your breath escape calmly and gently. Don't concentrate on your breathing so much anymore and feel your body, feel how earth's gravitation draws you more and more firmly into your chair or the ground.

Feel the pleasant heaviness of your body. You become very calm and serene ... and the relaxation becomes deeper and deeper. You are now very calm and deeply relaxed ... you are serene.

Imagination training

Repeat those words to yourself until you really become calm and feel a deep inner relaxation.

c.) Imagination training

(Pause for ten to 30 seconds after each suggestive prompt to allow images to form in your mind. These pauses are indicated in the first section by the rows of three or six dots)

Today:

Think of your breakfast. ... ...

Be as specific and accurate as possible. How did the things you ate taste? Close your eyes and think of the colors, not just of the food but also of the dishes you used ... the size and shape of the cup or glass ... What did you drink? ... What was its taste ... color ... consistency... temperature? ... Imagine the breakfast table ... the chair. ...

Think of any things that maybe you did not want to eat. ... Now add your recollections of the smells ... and sounds ... Was the radio on? ... the television? Was the cat purring?

Yesterday (pause as required, as in the exercise 'Today'):

Concentrate on an event that occurred yesterday and recreate the experience.

If you happened to get upset about something, let this feeling come over you again.

If you were happy about something, try to recreate the feeling of happiness.

If you spoke with someone, try to remember their voice, the color of their clothes, and the temperature of the place where you met.

Try to recreate in your mind the entire situation with all these details. Take as much time as you need.

The past:

Now delve a little further into your memory. Maybe you attended a celebration or a party, or had a particular success at work or an enjoyable experience in your personal life. Remember as many details as possible and try and make the images as lifelike as possible in your mind.

Tomorrow:

Now think of a place that you know, outside of your apartment or house, where tomorrow (or in the next few days) you will have something to do.

Imagine this place in all its detail: how it looks, how it sounds, how it smells, etc. Make these details as concrete as possible.

Future:

Try to imagine a place that you have not yet seen and do not know, but that you would very much like to see – maybe one day you would like to take a vacation there. Imagine yourself in that scenario: the clothes you are wearing and what you are doing. Mix in remembered images with the new ones you construct with your imagination.

Fantasy:

Think of something that does not (yet) exist and picture it in your mind: it might be your dream house, or a baby which has not yet been born, or yourself in ten years, or your first novel, or a sculpture you have made, etc.

Count backwards slowly from ten to one; on one, open your eyes breath in and out, deeply and slowly; stretch your body and do ten quick arm bends to make sure you are fully awake.

Paint an image in your mind or describe it in a book down to the smallest detail. Be as precise as possible and think of all of the particulars.

If you remember a particular tune or melody, keep it in your mind and, at the next opportunity, listen to this music in a peaceful situation.

After each fantasy journey, make sure you bring yourself completely back to the present; do not drive a car or conduct important business while in "fantasy mode."

After having done these preparatory exercises, we now come to the first actual fantasy journey and to the approach of the basal motives.

First fantasy journey:
"The optimal working day"

First
fantasy journey:
"The optimal
working day"

Let images of an optimal working day emerge within yourself. Images of a day where your expectations of self-determined duties were realized (it is easiest to ask somebody to read this journey to you. Otherwise read two or three suggestions or questions, then close your eyes again, relax, let the images emerge for a certain time, then open your eyes again and read the next paragraphs, and so on).

In any case, it is important to leave sufficient time between the image suggestions so that actual images can develop!

This particular day starts off with a great sense of naturalness. Everything is just the way it should be. Yesterday you fell asleep calm and relaxed, happy and content, because the important areas of your life fell into a wonderful balance.

Now you begin to perceive with your mind's eye and with all your senses how you woke up this morning. Your eyes continue to stay closed and, as if you are watching a movie, you see everything happening as if on an inner screen.

You now see the room with the bed that you have slept in. Is the room still dark or already flooded with light? What size is the room? Is it a bedroom? Did you wake up in a hotel room because you are on a business trip? Perhaps it is a room that you live in at the same time?

Take enough time to follow changing images also.

Is there anybody else in the room or are you waking up alone? What else can you see?

What furniture, what fabrics and colors determine the interior, the character of this room?

You now walk to the bathroom and after getting yourself ready you dress and find yourself at the breakfast table. Where do you breakfast? Now the images become so clear that you know whether you are in a flat or a house. Where is this flat or house? Look out of the window to create a picture of the surroundings – or are you already sitting on a balcony or patio overlooking other houses, are you looking into the countryside, over the ocean, or over a lake?

And after breakfast? Are you driving to work or do you work where you live? Do you work in a firm, at a clients, or in your own company or office? Again, allow enough time for the images that form to create a sense of harmony and inner joy within you.

*Then, all details of your working day become clear. Which roll do **you** play yourself, which other people appear?*

Who determines the work rhythm? Your clients, your boss, your team, or you yourself?

Which parts of the daily routine possibly still create stress, which ones create joy?

Are the contents of your work becoming clear? What task are you getting paid for? Who is acknowledging you and what for? How do you experience your own success, the feeling of being competent?

With whom do you compete? When and how is it fun to win? How big is your influence on events? Are you friends with your colleagues or are you just colleagues?

How do these images possibly differ from your actual situation at work?

And already it is lunchtime – time for something to eat. How, and perhaps, with whom and where, do you have your lunch? Do you have enough time for a quick nap, or a short walk down the road or in the park?

How does it continue in the afternoon? Do you continue with your work or do you have time for a round of golf, for the fitness studio, for inspiring conversations with clients, business friends, colleagues, or friends?

Are you a member of a club where you hold an important role, or even not so important role? Perhaps you need to prepare a speech or organize the catering for an event?

How and when do you finish your working day? Do you prepare yourself for the following day? What mood are you in, with what feelings do you drive home?

Can you now spend time on your private life? Or do you need to meet clients for a business dinner, think about a project, or prepare a trip?

What does it mean practically to you to enjoy your private life? What does a perfect evening look like? Again, let your mind run free here.

When do you become tired and go to bed? Tonight, you look back on the day contented and happy, and you fall asleep relaxed and calm.

When you are ready, count backwards slowly from five to one and make it clear to yourself that on one, you arrive wide-awake at that point where you started your journey.

On one, open your eyes; breathe in and out, deeply and slowly; then do a few quick arm bends, and write everything down that you have seen.

The best way is to write firstly onto the right-hand page of an empty book, so that on the left-hand page room remains for spontaneous thoughts or afterthoughts.

Now pay attention to the feelings that emerged or are emerging as you look back on your ideal working day. Write them down thoroughly also.

Spend time on the emerging afterthoughts and repeat this fantasy once in a while.

There is another guided fantasy journey to follow that has proven to be successful when making important decisions. You should, however, have had some previous experience with imagination exercises.

Second
fantasy journey:
"Making important
decisions"

Second fantasy journey. "Making important decisions"

Intensely practicing the ability to imagine can also be helpful when making difficult decisions. We took inspiration from Penney Peirce and Carol Adrienne (see bibliography) for the following steps of an imagination exercise:

Step 1:

Again, make sure that you won't be disturbed in the next 45 to 60 minutes (switch off cell phones, etc.). Sit or lie down comfortably and begin to relax more and more deeply, using a method of your own choice.

Choose three possible alternatives/professional options that you find worth pursuing. Clarify the alternatives and write them down on a piece of paper.

Step 2 (Read to you by someone or taped onto a cassette):

Start with the alternative that comes into your mind spontaneously.

Then assume that this option is already reality. Imagine step by step, in which surroundings you are, how you are behaving, and how others are now behaving. Imagine a new reality within which you move under new conditions.

Now pay attention to your feelings and emotions.

What do you feel physically? Which mental emotions and moods can you notice? Is it more a trace of being nervous, or do you feel full of expectations or excited?

Perhaps you stay very calm and serene. Or an uncomfortable inclination may develop, a certain heaviness or anxiety? It's possible that your pulse increases or your hands and forehead become damp. Stay calm and wait a little. The images will develop further and, therefore, so will your reactions.

Should you happen to like the first alternative, enforce the positive feeling and let the power coming from these pictures grow stronger and stronger.

Apart from the images, you may also experience impressions via your other senses. Perhaps you hear other people's voices or a known piece of music, certain noises. Or you smell certain odors. Enjoy a situation that is comfortable if it arises, it might even develop further into a state of real happiness.

Step 3:

Let your mind wander and move towards a period of time that lies approximately four to six months in the future. Do the sensations and emotions change? Do they change from relaxation to a feeling of tension or do they develop into an even stronger sense of anticipation? Imagine yourself completely in this state in the future. But just imagine yourself without thinking any further. It should remain a pure observation.

Step 4:

Now move further into the future, a whole year. Stay with what you can sense physically. Are there any changes; is anything reinforced or diminished? Does something previously uncomfortable now become comfortable? Or vice versa?

Finalization:

Wait for an inner impulse. It will tell you that it is time again to come back to today's day. Say good-bye to all images and sensations, impressions and observations. Erase them as if you would switch-off a light with a dimmer.

Take a few deep breaths, breathing out slowly. Feel how you move back into a normal emotional state.

Step 5:

Start the whole process all over again with one of the two other alternatives, doing it the same way as before. Afterwards, conclude with the third fantasy journey. Always conduct all four steps as well as the finalization completely.

Step 6:

Now take a little more time in order to clarify the three fantasies once again. But this time, create your associations in such a way that you stay strictly passive, where you don't become active at all. See the options in your mind's eye once again without any preferences. Does this passive attitude feel more comfortable or does it create tension or even anxiety? When you look into the future step by step, at what point do you feel the impulse to become active, to leave your passive role and to engage with the events?

Step 7:

Now return finally to the present and into the room where you actually are. Perhaps you would like to go for a little walk, listen to some nice music, eat something nice, or pamper yourself in some other way.

Only after a while should you go back to your decision-making. Select the option that creates a deep-seated feeling of coherence, and not one that merely removes an existing tension and that is easier to conduct. Count backwards from five to one silently. On one, open your eyes, breathe in and out deeply and slowly until you are wide awake again. (If necessary, do a few arm bends quickly to wake-up faster).

And finally, this is a fantasy that moves far into the future:

Third fantasy journey: "80th birthday"

You are celebrating your 80th birthday with a large group of friends and relatives. A good friend holds an after-dinner speech in your honor. What would you like this person to say about your life? Which of your acts and thoughts would you like this person to refer to?

Take a few minutes to visualize the course of your life. Don't force this process; just let the ideas and images come up of their own accord.

Then write down everything you have seen and heard.

(Another version of this fantasy journey develops when you imagine a TV or press interview to mark this birthday.)

Third
fantasy journey:
"80th birthday"

These fantasies are not meant to deliver a list of formulated values, but they can prepare you emotionally for becoming more sensitive towards your inner value system before you turn, in the next part, towards the cognitive (i.e., conscious) values.

The conscious motivational self-images that you can explore now on the next pages, are your *own associations, your opinions* about what is important to you. During your life so far, you have developed them step by step. On occasion, you have adapted them from desirable ideals; sometimes, they were established in opposition to other people ("I definitely don't want to be or act like that"). Some of them you adapted very consciously, many others have been integrated subconsciously. Therefore, the cognitive discovery process that we are about to employ requires a fair amount of investigation.

Little by little, you will notice more clearly in which areas the basal motives, on the one hand, and the motivational self-images, on the other, cooperate, coincide, and form powerful drives. And you will also notice those areas where, potentially, there is tension between the two motivation systems, and where it could result in a loss of motivation.

If, in such a conflicting case, you consciously decide to go with the values important to you, and not to go along with the basal drives, you should be aware of the fact that conscious motivation has to be supported by willpower and/or by extrinsic rewards. (More about dealing with your willpower from page 177 onwards; the list of rewards from page 262 onwards can provide you with ideas about this subject.)

B. Recognizing the conscious associations of one's own value system

Practical implementation:

Ask yourself what is especially important to you, what you want to have, what you want to experience, what sort of input you feel makes your life worthwhile. What makes your life meaningful to you? What could give you a sense of purpose? What makes you happy?

What gives you satisfaction? Which requirements have to be fulfilled in order to give you a feeling of delight or a sense of serenity, of inner peace? The procedure described here looks first at your whole life in order to provide an overview. (For more specific insights in different areas of your life see Appendix 1, from page 241 onwards).

Getting to know your own values system

Section A: "My important values"

Step 1: Overview of your list of values

Step 1: Which values are important to me: the values list

First, look at the values you have listed and select those that have a special meaning for you. Don't worry too much about whether you feel this list is complete or not. When you think about these values, let your mind wander; think about the experiences, hopes, and desires that make these values real for you. Some of them will immediately resonate with your experience, others less so. Some of them will already have an established place in your life, while others will be relevant from time to time, and others will seem to have no concrete relevance at all. Take some time to work through this process.

STOP

Values list A
(commonly cited values)

O Love	O Peace
O Comfort (emotional)	O Knowledge
O Marriage	O A home
O Health	O Ecology
O Recognition	O Honesty
O Mobility	O Dependence
O Solitude	O Calm
O Belongingness	O Charisma
O Helping others	O Sharing with others
O Children	O Popularity
O Freedom	O Appearance
O Power	O Security
O Closeness	O Composure
O Religion	O Leisure
O Critical ability	O Wisdom
O Adventure	O Astuteness
O Passion	O Success
O Rest	O Personality
O Flow	O Wealth

O Trust

O Solidarity

O Loyalty

O Family

O Order

O Creativity

O Punctuality

O Pleasure

O Individuality

O Fairness

O Influence

O Spirituality

O Fun

O Friendship

O Prestige

O Challenge

O Sustainability (ecol.)

O Comfort (physical)

O Self-expression

O Athleticism

O Independence

O Competence

O Belief

Step 2: Extension of your list of values

Now, supplement this list with values that you feel are missing from the list.

My personal additions to the values list:

O ————————————————————

O ————————————————————

O ————————————————————

O ————————————————————

Step 2:
Your own
additions to the
list of values

Step 3: Selection of the ten most important values

Now select the ten most important values irrespective of how much you feel they are being realized in your life at the moment. What matters here is finding out what is most important for you in your life. Do not rank these values for the moment. We will deal with that later.

3. Schritt:
Selection of the
ten most impor-
tant values

My current ten most important values:

_____

_____

_____

_____

_____

_____

_____

_____

_____

_____

4. Intermediate consideration: The difference between means and end values

Recognizing values of average importance

There is a fundamental distinction we need to make when identifying the values that are important to us

Take the value of love, for instance. Love is an ultimate emotional state, which we strive to achieve.

Family and money, on the other hand, are a different category of values to love. They are a means to reaching an emotional state.

A family, for example, can provide love, security, warmth, and happiness. When we see having a family as a value, we are actually aspiring to the feeling of happiness we obtain from the realization of these end values.

Thinking carefully about what is ultimately important to you can help you avoid confusing these two categories, and thus one of the most dangerous traps in life. Focusing only on intermediate values can result in the really important things in your life remaining unfulfilled and the empty feeling associated with the question of whether all the time and energy you have invested in realizing these values was really worth it.

Pursuing only medium-term values without being aware of the ultimate state you are aspiring to can lead to a great deal of frustration.

Means or end values? Test an example here. Assume that "money" is an important value:

What does money give me? Which end emotional values can I realize with the help of money?

_____

_____

_____

_____

_____

_____

_____

_____

_____

Intermediate consideration: The difference between means and end values

Continued over page

Another example: "Family"

Which end values can a family help me to realize?

_____

_____

_____

_____

_____

_____

_____

_____

Another of my own means values is:

_____

What can this value help me achieve?

_____

_____

_____

_____

_____

_____

Once you have identified which values belong to which category, mark the means values in your list with an **"M"** and think about the end values you are actually hoping to realize through these intermediate ones. This may lead you to expand and change your list of values. Only after going through this process should you move on to ranking your values (Step 5).

Step 5: Ranking your values

Now rank your values in order of importance from 1 to 10. Naturally the value that you want to realize above all others will come first, while the value you would abandon most easily if you had to will come last.

And be aware that the hierarchy of values you are putting together relates to what matters to you right now. You are merely cataloging these values. Whether you put them down in writing or not, the everyday decisions you make are being determined by these values unconsciously and instantaneously. Writing them down here means merely that you are helping yourself become aware of these internal processes of decision and selection.

"Life is about repeatedly setting out for the goal that you sense in your heart."
Irina Rauthmann

Our internal system is constantly engaged in actually achieving the states we aspire to. Determining the order of our values helps in situations when not all our values can be implemented simultaneously and the more important things have to be given preference over the less important ones (as is the case in nearly all situations in real life). Consciously observing this process might well cause you to smile (and it is important to be able to able to laugh at yourself), when you actually see what your internal system really finds important when you let it have its way. The values we assemble are usually formed quite arbitrarily along our path through life; we pick them up without noticing and suddenly they begin to determine our lives. You can assume that the present circumstances of your life are based on a value system that was formed around three to five years ago. Moreover, the value system that is driving you at the moment will determine the circumstances of your life in about three years from now.

"Important things must never be subordinated to unimportant ones."
Johann Wolfgang von Goethe

The highest priority should be given to end values.

You are today what you thought yesterday.
Buddha

Make an appointment with yourself.

Without wanting to encroach too much of your own selection of values, we would like to point out that it will be helpful if the four or five most important values at the top of your list are end values.

Our value system changes all the time and after a few years – once you have repeated this process several times – it is interesting to look at your earlier values lists. This allows you to understand your own process of development, which will allow you to see in action what Maslow describes as the principle of the change of importance *(see Focus 1: Self-Motivation – locating the sources of your energy)*.

In our experience, it is useful to check these lists at least once a year. And when you are beginning this process, it is probably a good idea to check your list after six months to see what developments you have undergone.

Use your diary to make an appointment with yourself to take up this work again. Many of the people attending our seminars use "the days between the years," meaning the time between Christmas and New Year's Eve.

(As we continue this process we will be assuming that the value system that you have identified corresponds to what you really wish for. You can obviously alter your value system at any time by changing the values or their ranking. We will be dealing with this later in Part II, when we look at possible pitfalls and how to overcome obstacles.

You are, of course, already free to enter new values in your list, to discard old ones, or to change their ranking, i.e., to take your fist steps in the process of change you are now embarking on.)

My current most important ten values are:

1. _____

2. _____

3. _____

4. _____

5. _____

6. _____

7. _____

8. _____

9. _____

10. _____

Date: _____

Follow-up _____

**www.
mypurpose.de**

Step 5: Creating a ranking of the ten most important values

Step 6: Defining and visualizing the degree of achievement – the Integrity Wheel

It is recommended that you produce a visual representation of this process in the form of a so-called Integrity Wheel (see Figure 11). This term derives from the fact that people who actually live out and experience what is important to them are seen by others as having integrity, as mature, at one with themselves, and as resistant to external influences. The integrity of a person and the individuality of his or her identity increases with the degree of realization of personal values.

Step 6:
The Integrity wheel enables you to establish the current grade of contentment

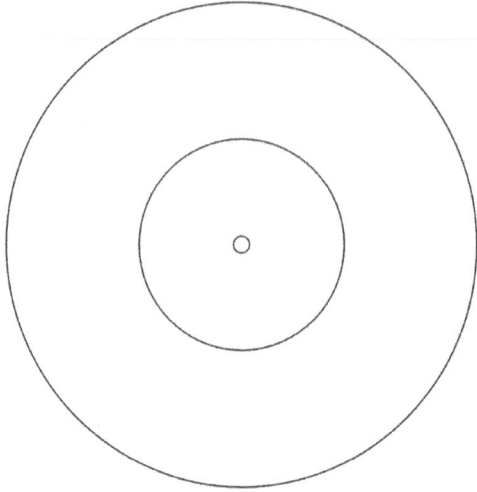

Figure 11: The Integrity Wheel (not yet filled out)

If you are not downloading your forms from the Internet, you should now make sufficient (enlarged) copies of the blank Integrity Wheel.

Only then should you divide the inner circle into ten sectors and enter the ten most important values (in any order you wish) into these sectors. Extend the sectors up to the periphery of the outer circle *(see Figure 12)*.

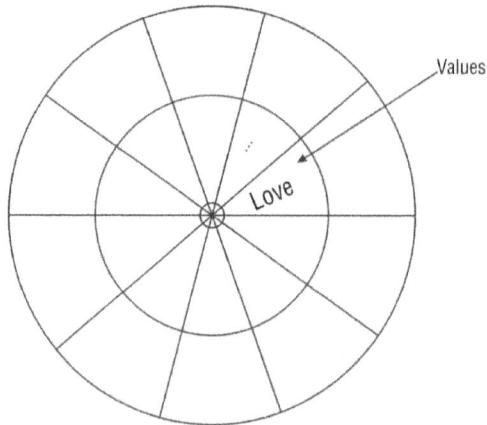

Figure 12: Example: Integrity wheel with the value "love." The other values should be entered accordingly.

Now look at each value and think about the extent it is being fulfilled in your present life situation. Rate this degree of fulfillment on a scale between 0 = "not at all" and 100 = "completely satisfied." Fill the sectors with shading or a color to illustrate this degree of fulfillment visually *(see Figure 13). (It is not necessary to be exact here. A rough approximation will do.)*

This process allows you to get a clear picture of your current motivational structure. Where your value is not yet fulfilled to 100%, you have a motive, a reason to work on increasing the level of fulfillment. As we saw in the first chapter, a motive is something that moves something in us, that moves us or makes us move something else to fulfill a need, to realize a value. A motive provides a reason for movement, a reason to do something in order to achieve a higher degree of fulfillment, of satisfaction.

Obtaining a clear image of your present motivation structure

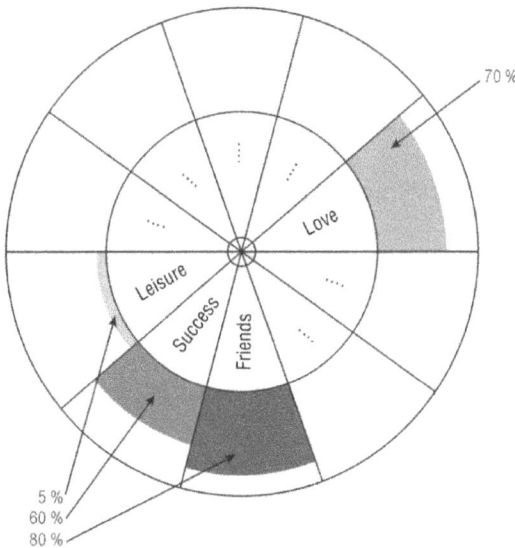

Figure 13: Example of a partially filled Integrity Wheel

Recognizing value deficits gives us the power to make changes, to personally grow. It enables us to find the energy to pursue important goals. On the other hand, sectors that are filled to a higher degree give us a sense

Personality: integrity and charisma

of our level of fulfillment, of the degree to which we are experiencing meaning in our lives. A person who lives out and experiences his or her value system to a high degree is generally perceived as a person with integrity and charisma.

Excellence rather than perfectionism

The wheel of integrity provides us with a picture of the extent to which we are approaching a life of fulfilled values and thus a life that is filled with meaning. However, it is vital here to *avoid the trap of perfectionism*. This process is not about ensuring that all sectors are filled out completely. As Maslow points out, this is impossible because the significance of different values can change over the course of our lives.

Of course, it should be our aim to fill out those areas we feel we can influence as far as possible, i.e., according to our abilities but not beyond them.

Recognizing the forces that drive us and *selecting* the ones we want to utilize: Wanting everything at the same time ultimately leads to getting nothing done at all

Our resources, energy, and time are limited, and we cannot expect to be able to apply all our energy in all these areas at the same time. Therefore, it is important that we pause from time to time and decide what we actually focus our energy on. Wanting everything at the same time ultimately leads to getting nothing done at all.

This process can take place in different time frames: short-term (immediate), medium-term (six to eighteen months), and long-term value realization.

Step 7: Focusing on the essential aspects – selecting two to three values.

Step 7: Selecting the three most important values: Start with a medium-term time frame of 12 to 18 months

This project will be easier to handle if you initially select two or three values you would like to work on in the medium term, i.e., over twelve to eighteen months. Mark these value sectors in your wheel with an arrow (*see Figure 14*).

Once you have built up some experience with this method, it is recommended that you repeat the whole process using a time frame of five, ten or fifteen years in order to begin working on long-term visions.

However, this is not to say that this process cannot be applied to the next six months, a single day, or even one hour.

The essence of self-motivation is gaining clarity about what is valuable to you personally and making conscious decisions about what requires particular attention, given the available amount of time and energy.

At this point, too, it is essential to point out that this conscious process should always take place while listening to your feelings, your basal motives (*"Is this the way of the heart?"*).

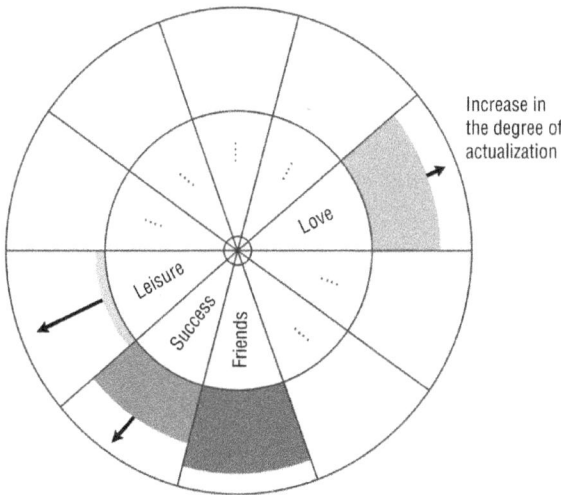

Figure 14: Selecting the values you want to work towards in the medium term (note that arrow in the "love" sector).

Step 8: Describing the meaning of the selected values

The next step involves describing the actual meaning your selected values have for you. The kind of terms we are using here to describe our values are words we use all the time, but how often do we actually think about what these individual values actually mean for us?

Step 8:
What significance do you allocate to your values?

Different people attach quite different meanings to particular values. Language is deceptive – it reduces the ambiguity of things.

In our work as trainers, we have repeatedly noticed that the terms making up our values list (p. 82 f.) are actually interpreted by different people in very different ways. These terms are merely labels. What makes them relevant to us as individuals is the specific meaning we attach to them. What do words like *"love," "freedom," "adventure,"* and *"success"* actually mean for you?

Now describe in one or two sentences what it would mean for you if a particular value were fulfilled to a much higher degree in your life than it is now. It is crucial that you invest a few minutes here before continuing with the process set out in this book. Take some time and make sure you feel relaxed before starting this short exercise.

Example:
Professionalism means for me that I listen carefully and attentively to my partner during consultations, and that I offer the services of my company in a way that suits the needs of the client.

(1st value:) _____ means for me that

_____

_____

_____

(2nd value:) _____ means for me that

_____

_____

_____

(3rd value:) _____ means for me that

_____

_____

_____

> *The description of the meaning we attach to a value that is currently not being realized but which we constantly aspire to realizing is, in fact, the same as the description of a wish.*

How our wishes develop

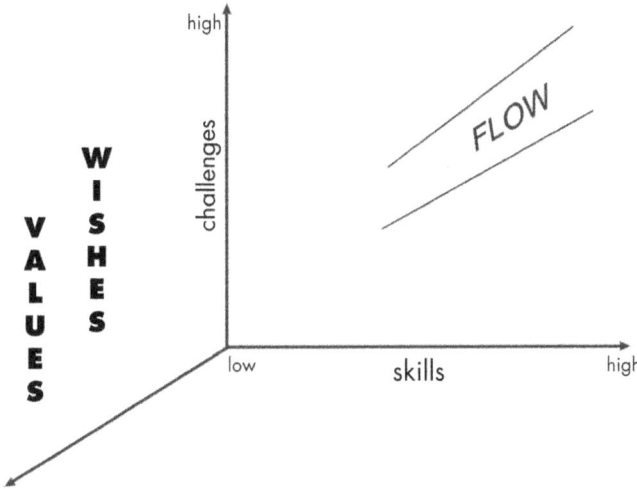

Figure 15: Realizing wishes – the Goal Scenario

Precisely describing what a value means to you and the extent to which you feel you have realized it enables you to crystallize your wishes for fulfillment in this particular area.

Step 9: Realizing wishes – the Goal Scenario

It would be hard to find a person who is happy without having wishes. Everyone has wishes. Yet only around five percent of people are able to turn their wishes into reality. The other 95 percent may well try at times to actively realize their wishes, but on the whole, simply live in hope. What makes the difference? What is it that distinguishes this five percent from the rest of us?

Step 9: Creating a Goal Scenario

People who realize their wishes develop images in their minds that represent the fulfillment of these wishes. They are able to use the visionary force of their imagination to generate a complex image, a whole scenario that charts the realization of their values.

Mobilizing the visionary force of our imaginations

They see themselves within this scenario and enjoy the idea of having already reached their desired goal. If they wish to learn a language, they do not simply think about how good it would be to understand and speak Italian. They see themselves in a stylish restaurant in Rome, in a spirited discussion with an attractive inhabitant of the city, talking about an opera performance in Verona on the previous day. Or they see themselves at an annual meeting of family therapists in Milan, enjoying the applause after a short presentation in Italian. Or they see themselves reading a healthy bank statement, planting an orange tree in their holiday home, or being given a post with higher responsibility in their company.

"Every time I see myself succeeding in my mind's eye, success comes to me more easily."
Liah Kraft-Macoy

It is important to create a vivid image of a personally experienced future in which what you currently see as an under-realized value, is envisioned as significantly more fulfilled. It is all about creating a Goal Scenario, the process of setting ourselves a goal, and the clear inner decision to actually direct our energies toward reaching this goal *("Commitment")*.

"Visualizing entails imagining something such that the idea becomes reality."
Shakti Gawain

To realize our own wishes, we require the following:

• a vivid, expressive vision of our target state;

• a written goal definition, a clear description or a visual representation of the Goal Scenario.

Wishes emerge from unsatisfactorily fulfilled values.

Goals help to realize values.

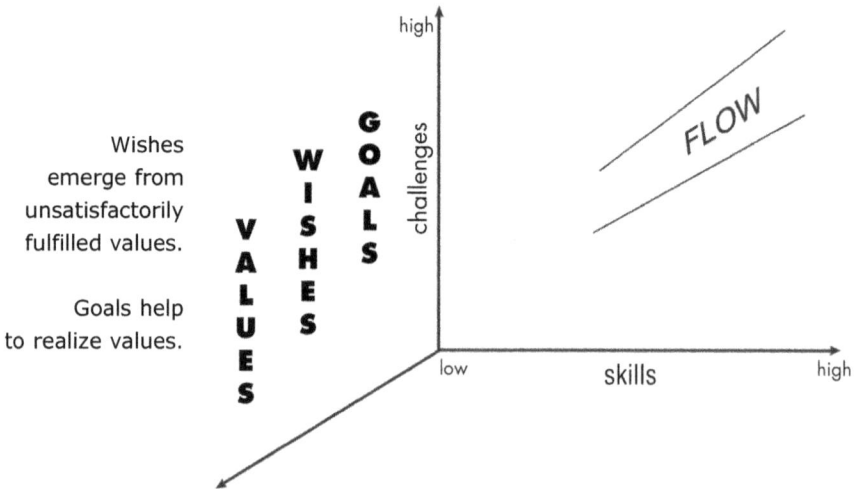

Figure 16: Realizing wishes through Goal Scenarios

We have now charted the process by which the flow space is "filled": from values (p. 65, figure 10) via wishes (p. 95, figure 15), to Goal Scenarios (figure 16, p. 96).

> *Due to the fundamental importance of the theme of designing a Goal Scenario we have devoted an entire chapter to it. See: Focus 4: The Goal Scenario (p. 103 ff.).*

Initially in this chapter, we managed to gain an overview of your complete value system with the help of the values list A1 (page 82 onwards). In Appendix 1 (page 241 onwards) you can, in addition, get an insight in to several specific areas of your life. There, you can find the individual respective values lists (B1–B6). The procedure is identical with Steps 1–9 that we employed for the values list A1 (starting on page 81). Hence, we don't repeat the introduction text in the appendix again. However, in the first column you will find a short checklist about repeating the procedure. When you work through the values list in Appendix 1 at a later point, you can then summarize the results on the following pages.

Here you can identify your values in more detail in relation to six specific life areas:

1. *Personal growth (personality development)*

2. *Profession, career, business*

3. *Personal relationships, friendship, love, partnership, family, home*

4. *Physique, health, sport, leisure, holidays, relaxation*

5. *Material well-being, possessions, wealth*

6. *Evaluation by others, prestige, recognition, social role*

You will find six more values lists from page 241 onwards.

STOP

When you have
worked through
the values lists in
Appendix 1
(from page 241
onwards)
you can write the
results in here.

**www.
mypurpose.de**

Overview of values you plan to more strongly
actualize in the future:

1. Values overview A: "all life areas"
   Here you can record (a maximum of) three
   values (see steps 7 and 8, p. 92 ff.)

   1. _____

   2. _____

   3. _____

Record only one value for each of the particular
life areas:

B 1: Personal growth, personality development

   _____

B 2: Profession, career, business

   _____

B 3: Personal relationships, friendship, love, part-
     nership, family, home

   _____

B 4: Physique, health, sport, games, leisure time,
     holidays, recuperation

   _____

B 5: Material well-being, possessions, wealth

   _____

B 6: Evaluation by others, prestige, recognition,
     social role

   _____

(1st value:) means for
me that

_____

_____

_____

(2nd value:) means for
me that

_____

_____

_____

(3rd value:) means for
me that

_____

_____

_____

(4th value:) means for
me that

_____

_____

_____

(5th value:) means for
me that

_____

_____

_____

(6th value:) means for
me that

_____

_____

_____

**www.
mypurpose.de**

»One of the most amazing things to me
is the way that new ideas and opportunities come
to those who decide
what they want
and have the courage
to pursue it.

It's the closest thing to real magic that I kow of.«

Michael LeBoeuf

The typical quality of creative ideas is as follows:

»First you give life and action, and guidance to ideas,
then they take on power of their own
and sweep aside all opposition.

Ideas are intangible forces,
but they have more power than
the physical brains that give birth to them.
They have the power to live on after the brain
that creates them has returned to dust.«

Napoleon Hill

Focus 4: The Goal Scenario
– the concentration of forces

"People are not lazy. They simply have impotent goals – that is, goals that do not inspire them."

Anthony Robbins

The real secret of self-motivation is revealed as soon as we understand the differences between wishes and goals.

An example of a wish is the desire to be an excellent athlete. An example of a goal is aiming to win the gold medal in a particular discipline at the Olympic Games in year X.

Goals are descriptions of future states that we regard as personally worthwhile. In contrast to wishes and ideals, goals are concretely achievable. We can wish to be healthy, wealthy and happy, self-confident, sincere, successful, caring, kind, well adjusted, and wise – but we will never know precisely whether we have actually achieved our wish or whether we are still only on the way to realizing it.

In other words, wishes describe an orientation; they are the expression of what we regard as important and valuable. We experience their fulfillment in certain moments to a greater or lesser degree, but never completely. However, when we reach a goal, we know it. We can clearly see that what we set out to achieve three years, six months, or only a few weeks ago has become reality.

"Goals are the beacons for action."
Dietrich Dörner

Goals can be distinguished from mere wishes, above all, by the fact that the moment in which a goal is achieved can be identified precisely.

"In idle wishes, fools supinely stay. Be there a will and wisdom finds a way."
George Crabbe

We can see, and in some cases touch, feel, count, smell, and/or taste the fact that something we previously only imagined is now a reality. The significance of this distinction between wishes and clearly delineated goals cannot be emphasized enough!

Based on studies in the USA, Earl Nightingale has concluded that while all people have certain unfulfilled wishes, only around 5% of people pursue clearly formulated, personally defined goals. He emphasizes that there is a direct connection between the realization of our plans and having a clear picture in our minds of what we are aiming for.

"People tend to become the image that they create of themselves. They construct a reality and thereby become this reality."
Carole Maleh, Matthias zur Bonsen

It is only when we develop a clearly defined image from a wish that we are able to generate the energy and stamina (=self-motivation) required to transform that image into a new reality. Wishes rarely come true "by themselves." When they do, we speak of coincidences or strokes of luck. However, in the overwhelming majority of cases, achieving goals we have set for ourselves depends to a large extent on our own efforts. Moreover, on our journey to realizing these goals we often find we need support from other people and have to overcome external (and very often also internal) obstacles.

At the beginning of this book we talked about the importance of dealing with energy, information, and time. This is not a mechanical process in which a certain input leads to a certain output. It is a creative process that includes unforeseen and often surprising elements. When we engage in this process; we do not restrict our lives so that we have complete control over them, but we also do not passively resign ourselves to our "fate" and allow everything to be determined by other people.

This process is about constantly challenging ourselves, exploring again and again what Rollo May calls the "narrow scope between freedom and destiny" and summoning the courage and imagination to develop the opportunities open to us at any one time.

Above all, it is important here to understand that the concept of freedom not only involves "freedom from … " but also "freedom to …" Some people equate the formulation of goals with a restriction of their freedom to act. But what value does freedom have if we do not make use of it? If we do not sometimes actually make use of our freedom to make decisions, to commit ourselves to a particular course of action at the expense of other possibilities (it is no accident that the Latin root of the word "decide" literally means "to cut off"), then freedom remains an empty, abstract concept.

"No one is free who does not lord over himself."
Matthias Claudius

Focusing on a clearly formulated goal in itself implies a high degree of freedom, because it involves a real, experienced freedom, a conscious selection from the wide range of possibilities open to us.

Freedom means not only "freedom from" but also "freedom to."

This conscious shaping of our own experience concentrates our attention and our energies, and provides us with the power and stamina we need. In fact, it seems that human beings have experienced this creative power of their imagination since primeval times. And yet, it also seems the case that each generation needs to find its own language to convince itself of the validity of this approach to life.

In the beginning there was the image

Take some time to look at the next illustration. It shows a cave painting from Niaux in southern France, painted around 13,000 years ago.

Use a principle that was initiated 13,000 years ago.

Along with many similar cave paintings that have been discovered in France, the Sahara, and South Africa, this picture numbers among the oldest existing pieces of evidence of human activity.

The scenes portrayed in these cave paintings are often of hunting, of animals that have been brought down, with spears and arrows still protruding from their bodies.

In some cases we also find people portrayed as stick figures:

People who are meeting a challenge

Unfortunately we have inherited only the pictures and not the contexts in which they were created. We can only speculate on what moved the artists to record precisely this moment.

Figure 17: The "Bison with wounds" from Niaux (from the book by Louis-René Nougier Die Welt der Höhlenmenschen (The World of Cavemen), reproduced with the kind permission of Artemis Verlag, Düsseldorf)

Research is still going on to find out more about these early drawings. We will not dwell here on the various hypotheses concerning why our ancestors invested so much energy and skill inside a cave system deep beneath the ground. And yet it would appear that, on the one hand, it was the wish to capture a moment that was full of excitement and adventure. We might also speculate that the pictures served another purpose, that people in this time gathered in front of them prior to embarking on a hunt in order to prepare themselves for the future, for the danger that lay before them – to summon the courage and determination they needed to confront large, wild animals.

Of course, we can also imagine the needs that compelled our ancestors to enter into these struggles. A human being must be very hungry if they is prepared to risk their life in order to acquire food.

In these pictures success is either anticipated or recorded. But whichever interpretation we choose to apply, one fact remains true: the pictures manifest a scene of victory over a dangerous creature.

Using the foresight generated by the power of imagination, these early human beings hoped to influence their future, to shape their reality rather than simply leaving it to the blind force of fate. In their simple yet magnificent drawings they made the invisible visible: hope, struggle, courage, determination, as well as victory, success, triumph, repletion, provision for other members of their species, and ultimately, survival.

The ability to make ideas reality is one of the most impressive human traits. This ability makes it possible for human beings to survive in a hostile environment and to shape it with their will to create.

Whether we think of the first cave paintings used by people over 10,000 years ago to prepare themselves mentally for the hunting of wild animals, San Francisco's Golden Gate Bridge, Neil Armstrong's journey to the moon, the music produced from a small silver disc, or a painting by Picasso: everything was originally an idea in the mind of a person. Almost anything the human mind can dream up and believe in can be created and become reality.

Great goals awaken great energies – and greatness should be understood here as measured from the individual point of view. A great goal can be your own small flower shop, your own business, a newspaper article or a photograph that gets published. A great goal can be a successful examination, conciliation with an opponent, or coping with a crisis. It can be a newborn child in its mother's arms or a parents' initiative that successfully deals with violence at school.

"A man
without a goal
is like a ship
without a rudder."
Thomas Carlyle

The single-minded, unceasing pursuit of a personally important goal strengthens our self-confidence, and increases our self-respect and our feeling of personal worth. Without a goal we are like a ship without a rudder, or as the poet Carlyle put it: "directionless, lost, a void."

It is important to emphasize that when linking our feeling of self-worth with goal-orientated actions, we should focus exclusively on doing the best we can in the present moment, (i.e., not on achieving the perfect end result). *We should never make our self-esteem dependent on the ultimate attainment of a goal.*

"The ability to be
happy liberates
one, at least for
the most part,
from the domina-
tion of external
influences."
*Robert Louis
Stevenson*

It is vital to remeber that achieving our goals depends on a range of factors, some of which we are unable to influence at all. This means that if we base our feeling of self-worth on achieving the goals we set ourselves, we are, in effect, making our personal happiness dependent on external forces we cannot influence. We are talking about a process, and within this process we need to be able to preserve the sphere of our own personal happiness for ourselves. We need to be able to enjoy the pleasures of success along the road toward our goals – but also to admit failure and keep a lookout for new possibilities and approaches.

»detached
involvement«

Is it a way
of the heart?

Admittedly, this all sounds a little paradoxical, and we will be returning to this aspect of what Parikh terms *"detached involvement"* later in more detail. We will also examine the meaning of the phrase, *"The way is the goal"* – which is often misunderstood as a good excuse for not setting goals. The meaning of this phrase only becomes clear when we take *"the way of the heart."*

Why do so few people sit down and write out an important goal for themselves? Why do people usually give so little thought to their goals and their motivations and, instead, simply "keep on moving?" What is stopping them from shaping their lives in a positive and long-term sense?
It is not our intention here to embark on extensive research into the motivation of people we don't know. Perhaps such people have simply never had the oppor-

tunity to define a worthwhile goal for themselves. Perhaps they have simply not been aware of what it is necessary to do to find one's own direction, or of the inspiration and satisfaction that the realization of a worthwhile ideal can bring.

Whatever the case, what we want to do here is pass on to you, our readers, what our own experience has shown us regarding the transformation of a purely abstract wish into a tangible reality. In the first place, this means transferring something in our minds onto paper – from the world of the intellect to the material world. The following ten aspects of a Goal Scenario design will help you to make personal – private as well as professional – wishes a reality. They are designed to help you find the motivation – the reasons – to set something in motion. If you carry through the following process, you will be able to exploit one of the most powerful and still least utilized sources of energy in the world – the power that is dormant within you to motivate yourself. You will personally gain access to the magic of a force that, for over 10,000 years, has enabled human beings to exceed their limitations and realize greatness.

Life is – to make the invisible visible.

The work of Miller, Galanter, Pribram, and others, as well as the concept of psycho-cybernetics established by Maltz, enable us to describe the human being as a goal-realization system. Everyone has a success mechanism that inevitably steers them toward their goals. And it is the quality of our goals that determines whether we are happy or unhappy in our lives. Goals function as a kind of lighthouse that shows our ship upon the ocean the direction to the next harbor.

In a certain sense, human beings are goal-achieving organisms.

A life is composed of many individual hours and days. And the way that life is shaped is decisively influenced by whether we allow ourselves to be steered, or pushed, by goals that can be realized within hours or days, or bigger and more inspiring goals that we set for ourselves in the longer term.

Without internal images of goals providing us with direction, we are not only without orientation but, strictly speaking, incapable of action. Whatever we do, whether it involves turning the page of a book or developing a new product, we need to have already envisaged an objective in our minds, to have made a "plan." The clearer and more precise our objective, the more effectively our success mechanism works to produce corresponding results.

Why is setting a goal so important? Your life will take on increasing personal meaning only if you are able to combine good ideas with the capacity to realize them, for instance, when you belong to the 5% of people who transform their dreams into a tangible reality.

The Goal Scenario is essential for small day-to-day goals as well as to the more important goals that we develop from our values system.

The extra step taken by people whose wishes become reality is a small but decisive one. The additional effort they make involves *envisioning a specific part of their future clearly and precisely* and describing this visual **Goal Scenario** in written form. Although it may sound simple to *"put down a goal in black and white,"* things tend to seem more difficult when you are facing a blank sheet of paper. And yet without this ritual of committing things to paper there would be no houses, no means of transport, and no more than the simplest of foods.

Let's look once again at the essential aspects of formulating and working with a Goal Scenario:

- Developing an idea of what you want on the basis of your value system

- Compressing this idea into a clear, concrete image – the Goal Scenario

- Applying your own talents, experiences, skills, and interests to a problem or a task

- Recording this in written or pictorial form

- Regularly reading what you have written and visualizing it (or looking at the picture you have drawn) until it develops its own dynamic and the idea takes on form.

Developing a Goal Scenario

How do we formulate goals that we find exciting and inspiring? We would suggest the following approach. Take some time to sit down and, with your eyes closed, imagine a successful scenario for your life. This scenario could, for example, be quite precise regarding the next three to five years, and then a little vaguer for the following period – say, the next ten to fifteen years. In this scenario, all your really important ideals become reality; your wishes and needs – material, financial, emotional, psychological, physiological, and spiritual – are realized and fulfilled

A look into your own future – activates the creative power of your imagination – it's always more exciting than reading your horoscope.

When asked about their goals, many people respond by listing the negative aspects of their lives they would like to change: *"I would like not to have this job," "I would like it if my mother-in-law didn't interfere so often," "If only I didn't have this boss . . ."* However, if they are asked what they would actually like, the response is often a long pause. It is clearly not easy to formulate the positive things we would like to introduce into our lives, and it is therefore important that you take your time with this task!

It is better to light a candle than to complain about the darkness.
Chinese saying

If you are not prepared to wait for a mysterious stranger to knock on your door and offer to fulfill your wishes, then you have to become your own magician. Your "magic formula" is quite simple: based on your personal wishes, start visualizing concrete future scenarios for your life and write them down.

Whereas the last chapter was concerned with the process of defining a number of fundamental wishes based on your value system, what we are concerned with here is the realization of these wishes.

How do you formulate your Goal Senario?

A very specific approach is recommended when it comes to formulating your goals. If you observe these rules, they will help you muster the stamina and energy required for the realization of your goals. You will experience that awareness and a clear formulation of your goals have very real effects on your life.

Divide the work into two phases: first map out what you want to achieve, what you would like to obtain, experience, or discover.

In the second phase (see p. 127 ff.) you should identify what you are willing to give, what talents, experiences, skills, interests, aptitudes, and specific features of your person you are prepared and able to invest in this process. And if we talk about a professional goal? In what ways are you particularly competent to solve problems for others? In what areas can you solve tasks that others find more difficult than you? What sort of bottlenecks could you eliminate that are negatively affecting other people, organizations, or enterprises, or that you can identify in your own enterprise?

The following diagram clearly illustrates the interconnected character of the process we are dealing with. Taking the example of professional life, the diagram shows the connections between the person as individual system and the larger enterprise system in which the person works. In the lower part of the diagram we have included a rough sketch of the still larger market system into which the enterprise must integrate itself in order to be able to sell its products and/or services to other people or enterprises.

If you want to gain something from another system, you need to produce an appropriate output, for instance, offer something useful, generate satisfaction, or make an artistic, creative contribution that is perceived as input and accorded an appropriate value by others. The other system will then be prepared to generate an output itself (in the professional sphere this takes the form of payment, vacations, bonuses, further training possibilities, career opportunities, security, etc.).

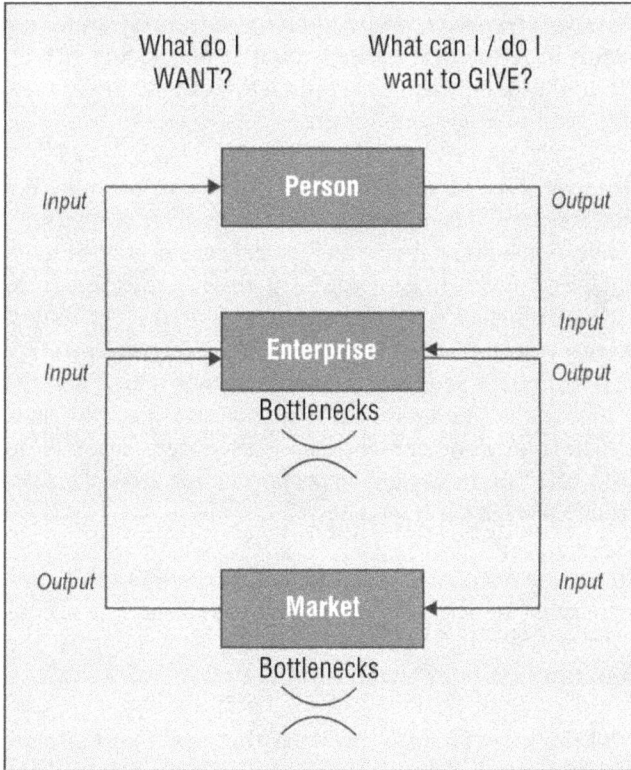

Figure 18: The person as a system within systems (based on Wolff, Frank, Mewes)

However, you can also apply this kind of system model to other areas of life (with appropriate modifications). Design a system diagram corresponding to your own specific situation. It is important to note that our diagram should only serve as a guide and can be modified to suit your particular situation.

For example, if you would like to design a Goal Scenario in the B 4 area (physique, health, sport, games, leisure time, holidays, recuperation) you could begin by clarifying the system constellation linking a healthy body with your own person. Instead of the terms in our diagram you can use words such as "physique," "health," or other concepts appropriate to this context. You can then develop precise ideas regarding what you expect from your body or how healthy you want to be, and also clar-

Advice on abbreviating the procedure:
In many day-to-day situations your potential contributions are obvious. When you want to do something for your body (see values list B4, Appendix 1, page 252 onwards), you will ask yourself directly what is sensible and what suits you. You can then skip the procedure described on pages 136 to 154 and **continue** immediately **on page 154**, formulating the Goal Scenarios. (When reading the book for the first time, you should at least acknowledge those pages briefly so that the meaning of the following becomes clear)

ify what you are prepared to do for your body and your health in terms of exercise, training, diet, living habits, etc. In these rare case you could leave out the lower rectangle in the original diagram.

However, if you want to develop Goal Scenarios in the B 3 area (personal relationships, friendship, love, partnership, family, home life) a three-level system constellation is more suitable: individual (i.e., you) – partner – partnership. In such a constellation it is important to note that the output you generate not only affects the second level corresponding to your partner and/or children. Both your output and the output of the second system level will also affect the third system level, in other words, the partnership. This will, in turn, result in further inputs on the left side from the partnership level to the levels above.

The system context represented here illustrates two principles, which – although perhaps difficult to accept – universally hold true and cannot be ignored in the medium or longer term:

1st Principle: There is no such thing as *something for nothing!*

2nd Principle: First *output*, then *input*

The second principle, which follows from the first, places greater emphasis on the importance of the correct order of thought and action. It argues that the idea of wanting to warm yourself by the stove before collecting the firewood just **doesn't work**. Producing heat always requires that you *first* cut the wood (often with numb fingers). Jails are full of people who have tried this in the reverse order.

Or as a Spanish saying quoted by Sprenger puts it, *"Do what you want, said God, and pay the price."*

After these preliminary thoughts, we can now get back to putting theory into practice. When working out a Goal Scenario in written form a number of aspects must be kept in mind, and these are listed below. We

Make an appointment with yourself.

are not dealing with a simple exercise here. You need to set aside time and give this task your full attention. Take two or three hours during which you will not be disturbed and find a comfortable environment to work in. Then consider the following:

Phase 1: What do I WANT?

Aspect 1: **Make sure that you are clearly aware of the purpose of achieving your goal**

Before formulating any Goal Scenario – whether at the individual level, in the professional or private sphere, or in relation to an organization or business – it is important that you are clear about the value system and the specific value or sum of values that form the basis of a particular goal.

If you have worked through the previous chapter, you will be familiar with the importance of describing the meaning of a value that is, at present, not being adequately realized, experienced, or lived out, and that you (or your firm) would very much like to see realized to a greater degree ("Formulating a wish," see p. 94 f.).

It is highly recommended that you actually work through Focus 3, "Values – recognizing the forces that drive us," beginning on p. 57ff., before you begin with the Goal Scenario.

Aspect 2: **Establish your goal in writing**

Write out the goals that you want to set in each important area of your life: your profession, your personal development, your relationships and private life, your physical, mental, and material well-being, and/or your relationship to those around you and their relationship to you. Be aware that it is people's unwillingness to make the effort to actually put down their Goal Scenario on paper that ultimately results in lack of success, inner dissatisfaction, tensions, and lack of motivation.

If you have a clear idea of what you aspire to but are unable to write it down or concretely represent it visually, you should ask what is causing you to sabotage yourself:

- Is this goal not really my goal? Is it perhaps not a "way of the heart?" Perhaps you have selected a goal that does not correspond to the value you have identified. In this case it makes sense to look for an alternative.

- Are there deeper reasons preventing me from actually reaching my goal?

If you suspect this is the case, then you should look closely at the obstacles to goal realization and how to overcome them (see p. 203 ff.). You may find that value conflicts or opposing fundamental convictions are playing a role here, and it is important to critically analyze these before you resume the pursuit of the goal.

Aspect 3:   Formulate a self-reference

Refer your goals quite concretely to yourself by beginning your formulation with the word "I."

Aspect 4:   Use a word of action that expresses your enthusiasm

"Flaming enthusiasm, backed by horse sense and persistence, is the quality that most frequently makes for success."
Dale Carnegie

Use a word or describe a feeling that expresses your enthusiasm for your Goal Scenario. Maybe you find the word enthusiasm a little over the top. The important thing is to try and a get a sense of the feeling you will have when the Goal Scenario is realized. You might want to visualize a series of images in the form of short film clips or video sequences of the situation you want to achieve.

Take the example of seeing yourself doing the kind of work you have always wanted to do. This is a reason to be happy and you should therefore write it down. Or you see yourself planting the first cherry tree in your own garden, or receiving the degree marking the end of your studies. Whatever it is that makes you feel happy, imagine that feeling and describe it in writing.

You now have on your page something like "I'm really pleased that ..." or "I'm so happy that now I ..." or "I'm completely fascinated by the fact that ..." Or if you're younger, you might have something like "It's totally phat or cool that ..." or something equivalent.

The main thing is that you find a formulation that precisely corresponds to your own feeling for language and gives you to a genuine thrill when you envisage that your desire has actually become reality.

Aspect 5:   Formulate your goal in the present tense

The thing that distinguishes your Goal Scenario from all other wishes is that it involves the formulation of a concrete task for your brain. For this reason you should use the present tense when you formulate your goal. If you write, "I am going to do such and such ..." you are, in fact, projecting the realization of your goal into an undefined future. The future is no longer concrete but abstract and not really tangible.

It is probable that the division of tasks between the two hemispheres of the cerebrum plays a role here. For some 90% of people in our culture, linguistic definition and the chronological arrangement of time are primarily activities of the hemisphere dealing with language (usually, but not always, the left hemisphere).

The other half of the cerebrum, which works with images, can recall the past and develops hopes and fears regarding the future, but its function is tied to the present. It can do little or nothing with a sentence such as "I am going to ..." For most people, such a sentence exclusively addresses the linguistic half of the cerebrum. Although this part of the brain can attempt to reach the specified goal, the process involved is a very strenuous one. For most people, it is the non-linguistic part of the brain that is able to access emotional-processing centers and the powerful neural structures that link these centers with the underlying limbic system, thus creating a network that delivers the motivational energy required.

It is therefore vital that we incorporate our "emotional side" in this process. Goals that we aspire to with both sides of our cerebrum are significantly easier to realize than those we work on using only our rational, logical faculties. A sentence formulated in the present tense switches on the areas of your brain that generate energy and mobilize your emotional intelligence.

Aspect 6:   Formulate your goal in positive terms

And now a particularly important piece of advice:

Formulate your goal in positive terms! Your formulation should, **on no account**, include negations, since these are only understood by the linguistic side of the brain. The areas of the brain that should be addressed by the Goal Scenario, the emotional areas of the non-linguistic brain, do not have the capacity to process words like *"not," "without," "none," "free of,"* or composite words using *"un-,"* etc.

These negations do not reach the non-verbal half of the cerebrum, so that if you do not observe this rule it is quite probable that you will achieve exactly the opposite of what you intended. You should, therefore, check the written description of your goal once again to ensure that it is expressed in positive, affirmative terms.

Aspect 7:   Make the moment of achieving your goal recognizable

The description of your Goal Scenario should be highly visual, vivid, and, above all, specific in *terms of quality* and *quantity*, and it should include a reference to you. This means that the way in which the scenario is plotted and the concrete details of the envisaged goal need to be presented so specifically that you will later be able to recognize the precise moment when the goal has been reached, in other words, when the description becomes a reality. Psychologists refer to the degree of recognizability described prior to reaching a goal as *"operationalizability."* As we have already emphasized, it is this factor that distinguishes mere wishes from goals. On the day we make our Goal Scenario a reality, we realize that we have now arrived at something we previously only imagined, because we can *see it or touch it, feel it, count it, hear, smell, or taste it.*

How does your goal taste?

And to ensure that you do not place limits on yourself, you are free to add the words *"… and more"* when describing the kind of quantities you aim to achieve.

It is evident from numerous cases that there is a peculiar, inexplicable connection between the clarity of the envisaged goal and the speed with which this goal is realized. It is therefore worth investing some time in the description of the Goal Scenario. This is why we suggest that you set aside at least two or three hours in which you can work on the details of your formulations without being disturbed. Choose somewhere to work on your scenario where you feel at ease, treat yourself to a cup of tea or coffee or a healthy fruit juice and let yourself be inspired.

Aspect 8: **Set a precise date (or one that is as precise as possible) for the realization of your goal**

Decide exactly when you want to (and are able to) achieve your goal and write this date down. Be realistic in your estimation; do not be too pessimistic but be careful not to be over-optimistic. If you see yourself reaching your goal in a too-distant future, it will lose its fascination for you. However, if you demand of yourself that you achieve all your goals from one day to the next, failure and resulting frustration are inevitable.

Rather than a fixed date in the future, you can also nominate a certain period of time, for example, *"… in the period between this date and that date."* And if you do not feel comfortable with setting a specific date, you can write: *"… at precisely the right time."* But do not assume that setting a date for reaching the goal will, in some mysterious way, guarantee that your goal will be realized at precisely this time.

It may be that your goal is indeed reached at this time, it may be reached far more quickly, but it may also take far longer than originally planned. There are simply too many factors that play a role in the realization of a goal and over which we have no influence at all.

Aspect 9:   Remain realistic

Remember the flow channel and do not catapult yourself into the realm of excessive expectations: Goal Scenarios should not be utopian. On the other hand, the Goal Scenario must be attractive enough to actually draw you out of the comfort zone. The starting point of the enterprise you are engaging in should thus be open. The secret of happiness lies in the fact that the channel in which we experience flow is a very narrow one. Otherwise we would all be constantly happy, which would probably be no fun at all!

When you formulate your goals for the first time, it is important that they should be relatively easy to realize in a short space of time. The experience of success you gain in realizing one of your goals will help you to develop greater trust in yourself and to realize the goals you aspire to. Armed with this trust in yourself, you will be able to make your subsequent goals more ambitious and to walk the path between the possible and the impossible. Experience has shown that a period of 12 to 18 months is a reasonable time frame for this initial phase.

Here, too, it is a question of practice. After a number of practical experiences you will find it easier to calculate the period of time that balances the fascination of the envisaged goal with the danger of over-estimation.

It is important that in some part of yourself you are able to believe in the realization of your Goal Scenario. But it is also important that your Goal Scenario has something a little "crazy" about it so that it really mobilizes you. Admittedly, this sounds a bit contradictory, but this is how the emotional right side of the brain functions, and it is from this source that we ultimately draw the energy we need.

– and avoid unnecessary stress:

People experienced in formulating goals tend to use descriptions that specifically guard against unnecessary stress, such as: "I will achieve this in a way that is easy, serene, harmonic, healthy, and positive for everyone involved."

Protection against too much stress: I achieve this in a way that is easy, serene, harmonic, healthy, and positive for everyone involved.

Aspect 10: Pay attention to clarity and consequences

You should also think about the fact that realizing a goal will also change the world around you. Use your imagination to envisage the realization of your goal as precisely as possible and ask yourself whether everything is as you would want it to be (see also *"Ecology Check"* p. 156).

If the realization of the goal or the pursuit of a particular goal has consequences for others, draw up a list of the people and the consequences involved. List the individual persons on one side and to the right of each name note whether the effect on the person will be positive or negative. In this way you are preparing yourself to deal with obstacles and to gain allies and supporters.

In the case of an important project, it is worthwhile making several notes about each person who has something to do with the realization of the goal, describing the consequences in detail, and the possible or necessary ways of dealing with this person (see p. 123).

People can react very vehemently if they are not informed or included in good time, and they can be extraordinarily helpful and supportive if they are given the necessary trust in advance.

It is essential that you do not use this method to manipulate somebody. For both ethical and quite pragmatic reasons you should never even consider using a Goal Scenario to tie another person to yourself or rope them in to the realization of certain goals. In the worst case it might even come to

Who is involved?	Consequences: (+) Advantages (−) Disadvantages

www. mypurpose.de

fruition, but what then? What can you expect from a partner whom you have won over in this way? This person will have no choice but to defend themselves with all their strength against this entanglement in another energy system. In the description of a goal you can outline the reality you desire in as much detail as possible by including type, height, eye and hair color, interests, personal qualities, and professional qualifications, etc. But do not list names or information that exclusively identify a particular person. Leave the identity open.

A shared Goal Scenario can be very powerful!

This is only relevant in cases where the person concerned is not aware of your project of goal realization. On the other hand, if you have an open, trusting relationship, or a comparable level of openness with another person, and you can envisage increasing the level of commitment or shared projects, then it is, of course, quite feasible to develop a shared Goal Scenario. Goal setting that is developed by two or more people is particularly powerful and these people are naturally able to overcome obstacles much more easily.

Consequences of realizing the Goal Scenario for:

Surname, first name

_____

_____

_____

_____

_____

_____

My possible or necessary ways of dealing with these consequences

_____

_____

_____

_____

_____

_____

_____

_____

_____

**www.
mypurpose.de**

But do not underestimate the difficulty of actually developing concurring wishes from two or three value systems and then a congruent Goal Scenario that all participants will pursue with the same feeling of commitment. You should only decide to develop shared Goal Scenarios with one or more people if you already have a strongly positive feeling in advance, and if you know the person or persons so well that you can assess their value system with a fair degree of reliability.

Aspect 11:   Trusting and letting go: changes are possible at any time

You need to develop perseverance and stamina if you want to realize your goal. However, it is important that this does not lead to a rigid attitude that causes you to persist at any cost. Trust in your own abilities but avoid becoming fixated and identifying yourself with your goal. And if you find yourself at a dead end or have other good reasons for abandoning a goal you have set yourself, or you want to alter specific formulations within the scenario, you should take the necessary steps. Abandoning a goal is not something you should do spontaneously but only after extensive consideration. If you then take this step, you should also give it an emotional clarity: by tearing up or burning your notes. In the case of alterations, corrections, or extensions of your Goal Scenario, you should always ensure that you have produced a satisfactory formulation of the new version before you destroy the old one. And here, too, the destruction of the initial version must have clarity for the non-verbal half of your brain in order to ensure that you really are able to separate yourself from the old ideas.

Trusting and
letting go
(see also p. 160)
More on this in
Part II, p. 177 ff.

Here is a brief example of a written Goal Scenario:

(This example only deals with phase 1. We will later return to the second phase, in which you formulate what you can contribute.)

For example, you have set yourself the goal of losing 5 kg by May 30. Envisage yourself as slimmer; try to imagine how relieved you feel, how mobile you have become, and how well you feel. "I really feel good about the fact that on May 30, at the latest, I only weigh xx kg or less. I have achieved this in a healthy, easy and pleasant way. When I look in the mirror I am much happier with myself, my clothes fit better, and the way I move is smooth and coordinated."

Or your goal is to conclude a contract worth 120,000 dollars on October 12. Envisage the signature on the contract and the handshake of your contractual partner. Imagine telling your colleagues and your family about the contract and celebrating it together. Every time you read your scenario out loud, envisage specific images corresponding to your goal – images that inspire you, make you happy, and give you the motivation and the energy to pursue your goal.

Practice exercise

Before you take on your own Goal Scenario, imagine you are someone who would like to conclude a deal worth 120,000 dollars on October 12. How might this person formulate his or her Goal Scenario?

_____

_____

_____

_____

**www.
mypurpose.de**

Phase 2: What can I, what do I want to, and what should I GIVE?

Achieving your goal will be more self-evident if it is clear to you why you will reach it, in other words, what you yourself are prepared to do to realize your aims. Being clear about your own contribution has the added advantage of providing you with the very positive experience of seeing that there is a whole range of good reasons for achieving your goals. These might involve the productive use of certain aspects of your personality or the application of particular skills that you have and which you can put to especially good use for others.

STOP

www. mypurpose.de

Have you already set a date with yourself to design and write down your goal scenario?

And don't "forget" Phase 2: What can I, what do I want to, and what should I GIVE? (see next page).

A model of a complete Goal Scenario can be found on pages 154 ff. – and on page 160 we give you an insight into Phase 4.

You will find advice on how to abbreviate the procedure on pages 55 and 113.

Checklist: Goal Scenario

Phase 1:   "What do I WANT?"

Aspect 1:   Make sure you that you are clearly aware of the purpose of achieving your goal

Aspect 2:   Establish your goal in writing

Aspect 3:   Formulate a self-reference

Aspect 4:   Use a word of action that expresses your enthusiasm

Aspect 5:   Formulate your goal in the present tense

Aspect 6:   Formulate your goal in positive terms (avoid negations!)

Aspect 7:   Make the moment of achieving your goal recognizable

Aspect 8:   Set a precise date (or one that is as precise as possible) for the realization of your goal

Aspect 9:   Remain realistic

Aspect 10:   Pay attention to clarity and consequences

Aspect 11:   Trusting and letting go: changes are possible at any time

Phase 2:   "What can I, what do I want to, and what should I give?" (see p. 127 f.)

Phase 3:   The complete Goal Scenario (HAVE and GIVE) (see p. 154 f.)

In both professional and private life the rule applies that there is no service without service in return. Apply this rule to all your goals. Ask yourself in the case of each goal what you can give – what benefits, stimuli, and joy can you offer other people, enterprises, or organizations in your professional life, but also, for example, in the interpersonal, cultural, and social areas. (And if your goal concerns your own health, ask yourself what can I give to my body, its organs, and its functions?)

Look again at the representation of the systemic con-stellations (see p. 113). After answering the question, *"What do I want?"* the next question is, *"What can I give? What benefits can I offer? What joy and enrichment, whether intellectual or material, can others gain through me?"* Or, for example, *"What can I do that is good for my body, my nerves, my heart, etc?"* This type of inquiry can be ap-plied to all six areas of life. Now focus your ATTENTION on what you can give others: your output.

Consider what personal strengths, gifts, talents, and skills, but also what aptitudes and interests you have, and think about your special features, those things that make you different from other people.

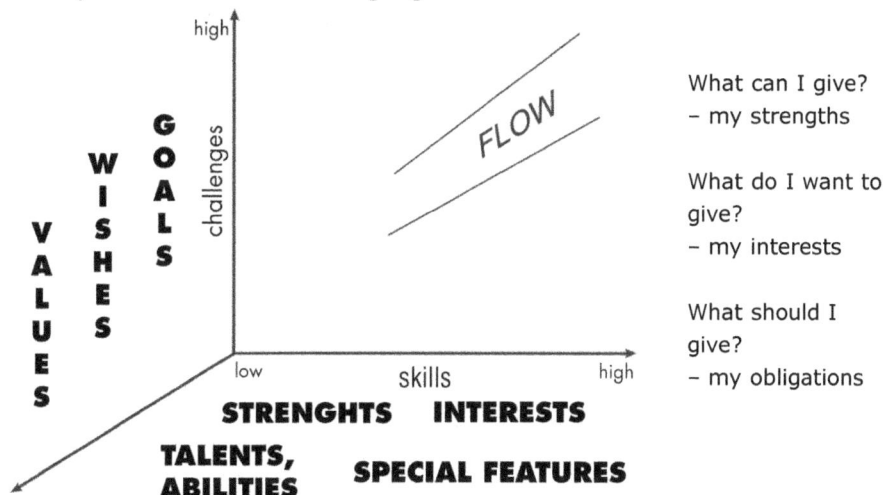

What can I give?
– my strengths

What do I want to give?
– my interests

What should I give?
– my obligations

Figure 19: The flow space and its basis: talents, interests, and special features

The next steps are designed to help you define your own uniqueness. This will enable you to precisely identify your point of departure, the point from where you have the best prospects of success.

Remember, you need to be clear on both the nature of your contribution as well as your preparedness to actually make it.

If up till now you have only worked on the "Values list A" (see p. 82 f.), meaning you have written out two or three important Goal Scenarios (see p. 111–126), then you should now decide which of the six areas of life (see next page) these goals should be assigned to.

The six areas of life are:

Six essential
areas in life
(for details see
Appendix 1, from
page 241
onwards)

1. Personal growth (personality development)

2. Profession, career, business

3. Personal relationships, friendship, love, partnership, family, home life

4. Body, health, sport, games, leisure, vacation, recreation

5. Material goods, possessions, wealth

6. Prestige, recognition, social role

STOP

**www.
mypurpose.de**

The first goal is in the area of:

_____

The second goal is in the area of:

_____

The third goal is in the area of:

_____

(If you look at the Goal Scenarios you have formulated, you will see that each of them fits into one of the six areas of life. This division will help you to precisely describe your contribution in the case of each scenario.)

The focus here is on identifying your particular strengths, the talents and skills you need to bring into play to realize a particular goal. First look at all six areas of life and decide which ones your first three goals belong to. If a goal fits to more than one area, select the area that requires the greatest level of commitment to realize your goal.

Consider whether these different goals can be simultaneously realized or whether there is a potential contradiction in the sense that realizing one goal presents an obstacle to realizing another. If this is the case, consider which goal is more important, which is easier to achieve, and which, if necessary, you should abandon. Sometimes it is surprisingly easy to resolve such conflicts by restructuring scenarios so that you can pursue your goals in a specific order rather than simultaneously. *Ambivalently fluctuating between two almost equally valued goals can be dangerous, because the result can be that you do not achieve either of the goals and end up feeling paralyzed.*

> Ambivalently fluctuating between two almost equally valued goals can be very dangerous.

Selecting the correct strategy

A strategy is the carefully considered application of the available resources at the right point in order to gain the maximum possible effect. You should ask yourself which strategy you want to employ before setting out to achieve your goal. Which resources are you able to employ? Which ones are you want employ? And how do you want to make use of them? We have now reached a decisive point. There are two very different ways of approaching the question of what you want to contribute toward, or invest in, the realization of a goal. These two ways are based on two very different strategies for leading life. This book is based on the strategy which involves proceeding from the foundation of your own talents and building up your

> Strategy I: Strengthening strengths.

strengths, in other words, becoming better and seeking challenges in those areas to which you are already well suited. Our own work as well as extensive empirical studies in Germany and the USA, confirm the success of this approach.

Strategy II: The compensation strategy – making a strength out of a weakness.

However, there is another quite different strategy: the compensation strategy. This approach involves taking a weakness (or even a handicap) and making it into a strength: this strategy can mobilize extraordinary energies, but it is dependent upon quite specific, personal prerequisites. However, since identifying these perquisites is better suited to the framework of personal consultation and coaching, we will not explore this strategy in detail here.

You gain strength, courage and confidence by every experience in which you stop to look fear in the face. You must do the thing which you think you cannot do.
Eleanor Roosevelt
s.a.:
www. mypurpose.de

If you feel that such a strategy is more appropriate, you could, for example, find inspiration in the biographies of great people who have overcome their handicaps. People such as Demosthenes (a renowned speaker despite having a pronounced speech impediment and suffering from extreme shyness), Wilma Rudolph (winner of the 100 meters and 200 meters relay gold medals for the USA in the Olympic Games in 1960 in Rome despite having suffered from polio and other serious diseases as a child), Helen Keller (writer, blind and deaf), Beethoven (a composer despite suffering from deafness), etc., provide examples of what people can achieve who make weaknesses into strengths.

Shortening the process:

However, we sometimes find constellations in which it makes sense to combine both strategies. You may also find it necessary in some cases to focus on correcting a particular weakness, because if it is not overcome you will not be able to apply and develop the talents and strengths you already have. However, in applying the strategy of strengthening your strengths and developing a deeper understanding of this approach, you will also become more aware of this weakness-strength relationship and how you can concretely deal with it.

See the marginal note on page 113.

Concentrate on one area of life and ask yourself the following:

Step 1: What are my strengths – my gifts, talents, abilities, and particular proficiencies?

You can use the following points as an initial guideline, although it is important that, above all, you identify your own specific gifts and talents. You should focus on those abilities which you have always had and which do not require an enormous effort to bring into play. It is here that your particular advantages are to be discovered.

At the beginning of this process of discovering your own talents and gifts, it is important to note that we are not so much concerned here with what you have learned to do at some point, in other words, the focus is not on things like being able to play the piano, but more on the qualities underlying this skill, such as *finger dexterity* or a high level of *physical coordination*.

You will gain greater clarity regarding you own specific possibilities and potential if you strictly separate your talents and gifts from your fund of knowledge, proficiencies, and experiences. Marcus Buckingham and his colleagues, who have conducted studies for the Gallup organization into the way people deal with their weaknesses and strengths involving hundreds of thousands of individuals, describe talents as *"recurring patterns of thought, feeling or behavior that can be productively applied."* In their view *"gifts are found in those things that one does gladly and often, that is, habitually."*

Using the following guidelines, make a list of all your gifts and personal abilities and then select the six talents and personal abilities that you feel are particularly developed.

To help you with this process we have compiled an extensive list of talents and abilities using a range of selection criteria. Take some time to study these and let yourself be inspired before making a definitive choice for your own strengths profile.

When you are making your final selection, concentrate on those strengths, which you would really like to apply in the future. You will find a prepared layout for your list on p. 148. (List of possible talents: p. 135 f.).

A. Identifying basic talents with multiple applications

a) What are basic talents with multiple applications?

Basic talents with multiple applications are abilities that you have always had and which potentially could be applied in a new variation.

It is important to explain what we understand by the term "talents." We draw here on the work of John C. Crystal and Richard N. Bolles, who have engaged with this question in a way that is both comprehensive and precise. If you ask a person what their strengths are, you usually receive an answer consisting of two parts. On the one hand, the person being questioned usually makes approximately six statements, such as "I'm good at solving problems" or "I get on well with other people." On the other hand, those questioned will also list the skills they have acquired in school or at other educational institutions (vocational school, technical school, university, etc.).

On closer consideration it seems that abilities can be divided into three categories:

I. Abilities requiring an effort, which is also noticeable to others.

II. Abilities requiring great effort and involving problems, which are not noticed by others.

III. Abilities that come easy to the person and which appear as such to the outside observer.

If you were asked about your abilities, you would probably first recall those in category I, then those in category II, and finally those in category III.

It follows that the greater the abilities of a person in a specific area, the less he or she perceives them as abilities. *We are more aware of the things that cause us difficulty than the things we achieve without effort.*

For example, your ability to touch-type with ten fingers might correspond to level I, your ability as a skier to level II, and your ability to write by hand to level III. If you were suddenly asked about your abilities then you would most likely first recall your capacity with a computer keyboard, then your ability to ski and lastly your ability to write by hand. This means *that the longer a person has been able to do something without having to make an effort, the more self-evident this ability has become and the less likely it is to come to mind when he or she is asked about his or her abilities.* In the case of certain very familiar abilities, one will not even be able to remember how long one has actually had them.

The greater the abilities of a person in a specific area, the less he or she perceives them as abilities – we are too familiar with our talents to notice them.

Once we realize this, a quite new approach becomes possible. First, we must ask ourselves whether these three categories really cover the full range of abilities. The answer is in fact no, because closer consideration reveals a fourth category of abilities:

IV. **The talents that have always been there and which you have been able to apply without effort from the beginning.**

The ability to use a typewriter or computer keyboard, for example, could be classified in one of the first three categories independently of the person being asked, but never in the fourth category.

This fourth category tends to include basic talents such as manual dexterity and a high level of physical coordination. It is precisely because we have always had such talents and have not had to learn them that we are not necessarily really aware of them. They are thus the ones least likely to occur to us when we are listing our talents. Yet it is the talents we are born with or which we develop when we are young that represent our greatest strengths. They are talents that we can apply most effectively and easily in our professional lives. In order to be able to identify the abilities that fall into category IV, we must now begin to make more precise and clearer conceptual distinctions. In the course of many years of surveys and evaluations for the Gallup organization involving more than one million people from 63 countries, Marcus Buckingham, Donald O. Clifton, and Curt Coffman have focused, above all, on *the identification of talents*. You can find detailed instructions on how talents can be recognized in the book *First, Break All the Rules* by Buckingham/ Coffman, chapter 7. The 34 talents necessary for your professional life are explained more clearly in the book *Now, Discover Your Strengths* by Buckingham/Coffman. On the third (inner) cover page of this book you will also find a code, which you can use to do a test – the so called "strengths finder" on Gallup's website (www.strengths finder.com), in order to find your personal talents.

"Talents are characterized by changelessness and *good feeling*." Buckingham, Clifton

Clifton Strengthsfinder ™ – Quick Reference Card

Achiever People strong in the Achiever theme have a great deal of stamina and work hard. They take great satisfaction from being busy and productive

Activator People strong in the Activator theme can make things happen by turning thoughts into action. They are often impatient

Adaptability People strong in the Adaptability theme prefer to "go with the flow". They tend to be "now" people who take things as they come and discover the future one day at a time

Analytical People strong in the Analytical theme search for reasons and causes. They have the ability to think about all the factors that might affect a situation

Arranger People strong in the Arranger theme can organize, but they also have a flexibility that complements this ability. They like to figure out how all of the pieces and resources can be arranged for maximum productivity

Belief People strong in the Belief theme have certain core values that are unchanging. Out of these values emerges a defined purpose for their life

Command People strong in the Command theme have presence. They can take control of a situation and make decisions

Communication People strong in the Communication theme generally find it easy to put their thoughts into words. They are good conversationalists and presenters

Competition People strong in the Competition theme measure their progress against the performance of others. They strive to win first place and revel in contests

Connectedness People strong in the Connectedness theme have faith in the links between all things. They believe there are few coincidences and that almost every event has a reason

Consistency People strong in the Consistency theme are keenly aware of the need to treat people the same. They try to treat everyone in the world with consistency by setting up clear rules and adhering to them

Context People strong in the Context theme enjoy thinking about the past. They understand the present by researching its history

Deliberative People strong in the Deliberative theme are best described by the serious care they take in making decisions or choices. They anticipate the obstacles

Developer People strong in the Developer theme recognize and cultivate the potential in others. They spot the signs of each small improvement and derive satisfaction from these improvements

Discipline People strong in the Discipline theme enjoy routine and structure. Their world is best described by the order they create

Empathy People strong in the Empathy theme can sense the feelings of other people by imagining themselves in others' lives or others' situations

Focus People strong in the Focus theme can take a direction, follow through, and make corrections necessary to stay on track. They prioritize, then act

Futuristic People strong in the Futuristic theme are inspired by the future and what could be. They inspire others with their visions of the future

Harmony People strong in the Harmony theme look for consensus. They don't enjoy conflict; rather, they seek areas of agreement

Ideation People strong in the Ideation theme are fascinated by ideas. They are able to find connections between seemingly disparate phenomena

Includer People strong in the Includer theme are accepting of others. They show awareness of those who feel left out, and make effort to include them

Individualization People strong in the Individualization theme are intrigued with the unique qualities of each person. They have a gift for figuring out how people who are different can work together productively

Input People strong in the Input theme have a craving to know more. Often they like to collect and archive all kinds of information

Intellection People strong in the Intellection theme are characterized by their intellectual activity. They are introspective and appreciate intellectual discussions

Learner People strong in the Learner theme have a great desire to learn and want to continuously improve. In particular, the process of learning, rather than the outcome, excites them

Maximizer People strong in the Maximizer theme focus on strengths as a way to stimulate personal and group excellence. They seek to transform something strong into something superb

Positivity People strong in the Positivity theme have an enthusiasm that is contagious. They are upbeat and can get others excited about what they are going to do

Relator People who are strong in the Relator theme enjoy close relationships with others. They find deep satisfaction in working hard with friends to achieve a goal

Responsibility People strong in the Responsibility theme take psychological ownership of what they say they will do. They are committed to stable values such as honesty and loyalty

Restorative People strong in the Restorative theme are adept at dealing with problems. They are good at figuring out what is wrong and resolving it

Self-Assurance People strong in the Self-Assurance theme feel confident in their ability to manage own lives. They possess an inner compass that gives them confidence that their decisions are right

Significance People strong in the Significance theme want to be very important in the eyes of others. They are independent and want to be recognized

Strategic People strong in the Strategic theme create alternative ways to proceed. Faced with any given scenar-io, they can quickly spot the relevant patterns and issues

Woo People strong in the Woo theme love the challenge of meeting new people and winning them over. They derive satisfaction from breaking the ice and making a connection with another person

c.) What Color is Your Parachute?

Another useful, pragmatically based approach is put forward by Richard N. Bolles, whose standard work *What Color Is Your Parachute?* (annually revised since 1970) is written for everyone who wants, or has to, look for a job. Bolles has developed a highly comprehensive and sophisticated system for identifying one's abilities. However, he too emphasizes that identifying these strengths is not enough in itself. It is crucial that we apply our abilities in contexts and ways that give us pleasure and a sense of satisfaction. He makes a fundamental distinction between three main areas in which you can rediscover your talents, depending on which of the following questions you ask yourself:

Would I like to apply my talents predominantly:

- in dealing with *people*

- in handling *objects and things*

- in working with *data and information*

B. Extension of your talent list by asking others

For any further indication on seeking your existing talents talk to other people, particularly people that you know well, and ask them what they find your specific strengths to be. Sometimes, a talent might be in your *blind spot*, which others have already noticed and are familiar with, but you yourself do not find worthwhile including, as you have been familiar with it your whole life. This may lead to potential talent not being utilized.

Then write all your strengths down into the box *"list of my strengths"* (on page 139).

You can keep adding to this list when, for example, other people who know you well point out strengths that you have, until now, been *unaware* of.

Now select your six greatest strengths, bearing in mind which strengths you actually want to apply in your professional life. You should primarily concentrate here on "talents," in other words, abilities that come to you easily.

Now record these six strengths and abilities in the "Give" Integrity wheel (see p. 141) in six fields in the upper left sector (see p. 140 for an example).

You now need to evaluate yourself in relation to each of these abilities. How well developed is each of your abilities? Is it average, less than average, or more than average? Within the "profession, career, business" life sphere, use the average qualifications of people who are in a similar professional area to yourself as a guide to your evaluation. (You can then apply this basic idea to the other life spheres and evaluate yourself accordingly). Here, we are concerned only with your own subjective evaluation. The middle circular arc represents the general average. The following illustration provides an example. Use this as a guide to record your own strengths in the empty Integrity wheel on page 141.

We will be extending this process of evaluation later (p. 146 ff.).

List of my strengths, talents, abilities:

_____

_____

_____

_____

_____

_____

_____

_____

STOP

**www.
mypurpose.de**

STOP

My six most pronounced strengths at present:

1. _____

2. _____

3. _____

4. _____

5. _____

6. _____

Select your
greatest strength.

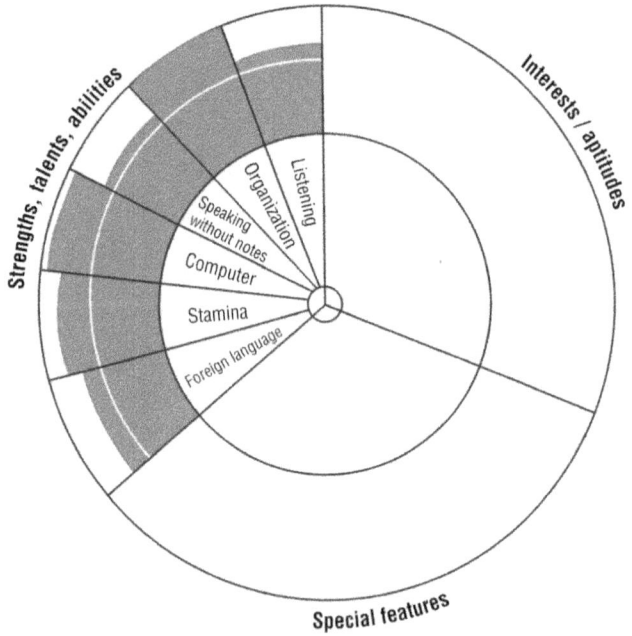

Strengths, talents, abilities

Listening

Organization

Speaking without notes

Computer

Stamina

Foreign language

Interests / aptitudes

Special features

Figure 20: "Give" Integrity Wheel: example of the selection and evaluation of strengths

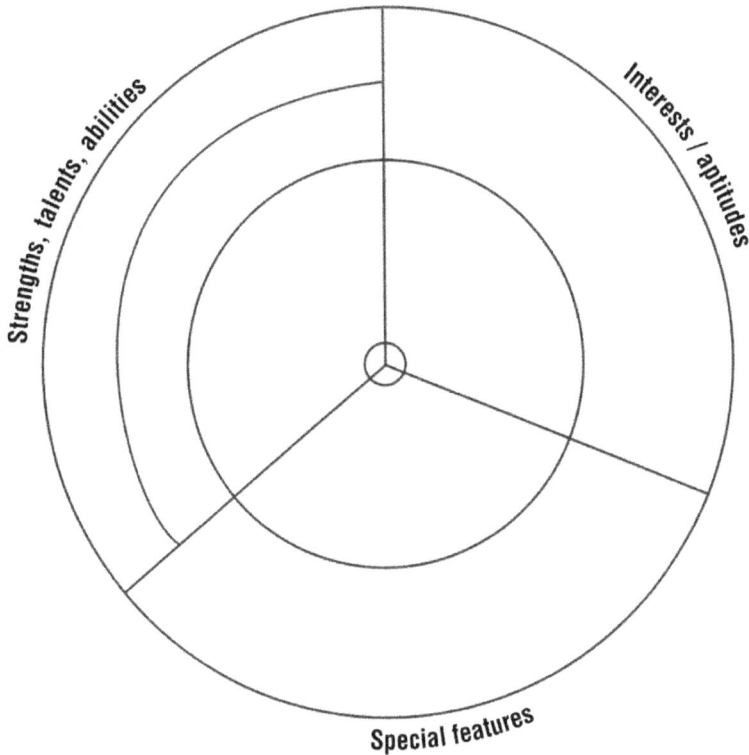

Figure 21: "Give" Integrity Wheel: layout for your own evaluation

Step 2: What are my interests and inclinations?

You now need to identify your interests and aptitudes in the relevant sphere. At this point you should also consider interests and aptitudes relating to other spheres, since you may find surprising combination possibilities. You do not have to make any definitive decisions yet. Follow your intuition and write down everything that occurs to you. Selection and evaluation will come later. Here, we are concerned with those activities that you enjoy.

We are not concerned here with enjoyment per se. You should select activities that give you energy, that give you a kick and recharge your batteries. There are a large number of activities which are fun to do but which leave us without energy and internally exhausted. Such interests should not be included here. (We are not referring here to activities that, while physically exhausting, have an effect that is intellectually inspiring and invigorating.) You should only list the things that give you an additional surge of energy. It is not relevant whether you currently engage in this activity or not. Perhaps in the past you have gone horse riding but you don't have time for this now. Yet you feel that you would enjoy it just as much as you did ten years ago. You should therefore write down "riding." *(An activity like this is a good example of something that is physically exhausting but intellectually invigorating.)* Simply write down everything you enjoy that you do not want to exclude from your professional life. (Your list may also include apparently trivial "passions" such as chatting on the phone.) Select a minimum of two and a maximum of six interests.

As soon as you have decided, record these interests in the second sector (above right) of the "Give" Integrity Wheel (see p. 141). Decide on the relative strength of each interest and indicate this strength with an arrow in the relevant sector, for instance, your strongest interest will be indicated by the longest arrow – your weakest interest by the shortest arrow (see the example in the illustration on the next page). Here, too, you can also consider asking for a good friend's opinion.

**www.
mypurpose.de**

Once you have gone through this whole process, you will see that the insights you have gained make you want to modify and revise these initial, spontaneous statements.

My six most pronounced interests and aptitudes are (to be entered in the "Give" Integrity Wheel, see p. 141):

1. _____

2. _____

3. _____

4. _____

5. _____

6. _____

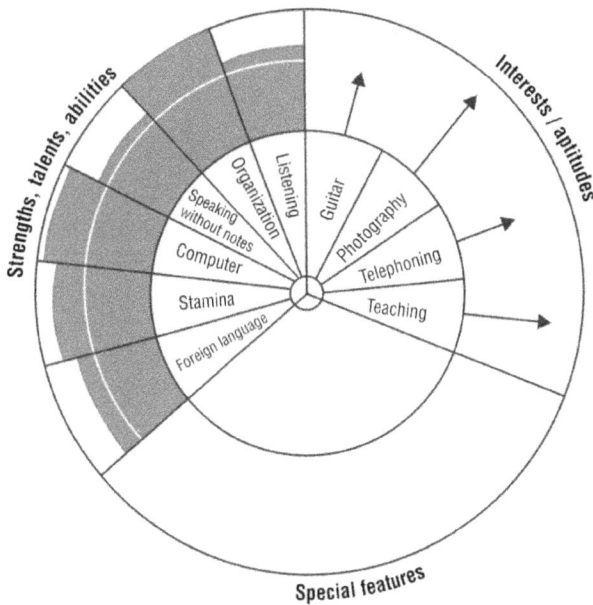

Figure 22 "Give" Integrity Wheel: example of recording interests and aptitudes (practical implementation see p. 141 f.)

Step 3: What are my special features?

In the third sector of the wheel you should record all the characteristics and features of your person or life that you feel distinguish you from other people.

These could be:

• *physical features*

– Do not confine yourself here to strengths. Weaknesses can also be special features. Don't be too hasty in your evaluation. Your task here is simply to recognize what distinguishes you from others. Wolff/Frank *("Professional Goal Identification")* refer to the example of a self-employed locksmith who had a leg amputated as the result of an accident. Rather then becoming embittered and resigning himself to severe disablement, this man became a specialist in the development of customized devices enabling amputees to drive. The result: a new group of car buyers. In short, a great success!

• *or psychological features*

– Numerous great works in the fields of music and of literature have been written by people suffering from what might be termed psychological instability. Such instability can be the key to particular creative achievements. We do not refer to *"genius and madness"* for nothing.

• *or specific biographical features*

– particular achievements, experiences – including negative ones – awards, public recognition, civil courage, bravery (e.g., saving a life)

and finally:

• *features of image/perception by others*

– effect on others. How do other people rate you, etc?

Now select between two and six "special features" and record these in the Integrity wheel (third sector in Figure 21, see p. 141). Then evaluate these features in relation to what you see as their frequency in the general population and indicate this with arrows in the corresponding sectors of the diagram. A feature that will probably be found in only a very small number of people (*e.g., a win of at least 100,000 dollars in the lottery*) should be marked using a particularly long arrow, whereas features commonly found in other people (*e.g., you wear glasses*) should be marked using a correspondingly short arrow.

After you have completed this self-analysis, you should again take the time to supplement, question, and possibly correct this image by asking people who know you for their assessment of these aspects of your personality (*"external assessment"*). In this way you can draw on the opinions of those you trust to establish an "external" image. It's a chance to take a look at yourself through others' eyes.

My special features are (to be entered in the "Give" Integrity Wheel, see p. 141):

1. _____

2. _____

3. _____

4. _____

5. _____

6. _____

STOP

www. mypurpose.de

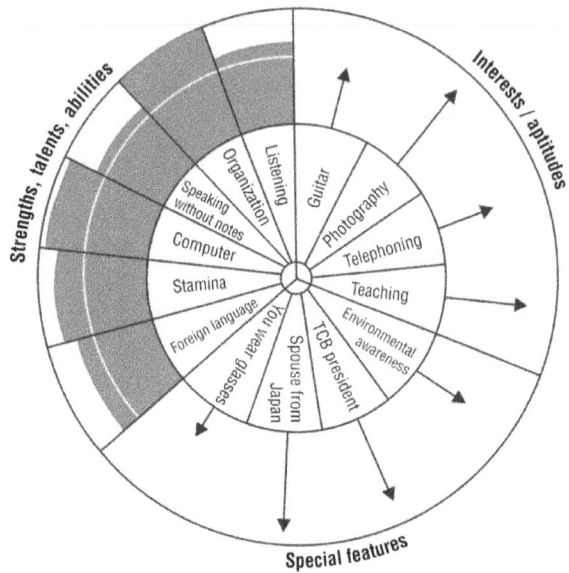

Figure 23 "Give" Integrity Wheel: example of how to record special features

Step 4: Evaluation

Since the strategy we are employing here involves *strengthening your strengths*, select the two most outstanding features in each of the three sectors and write these down one under the other (see p. 147).

You might find that this spontaneous evaluation produces quite surprising combinations, and you might start asking yourself if you are perhaps better suited to running a flea circus. It is important that you do not let your internal censorship mechanism take over here. Give your ideas free rein and write down everything that occurs to you (spontaneous evaluation A).

Once you have had a chance to reflect on this initial evaluation, to use it as a basis for further self-exploration and to gather external assessments from other people, you can revise the Give Integrity Wheel and formulate an additional "considered evaluation (B)" (Step 5, p. 148 ff.)

The leap beyond everyday patterns of thinking can be highly stimulating and inspirational. It is important to give this process time. Do not expect a comprehensive and informed answer immediately. More ideas will emerge in the coming days and weeks. *Engage in an inner dialogue and allow yourself enough time to do this.*

A: My profile
Strengths (talents, abilities, aptitudes):

1. _____

2. _____

Interests and aptitudes:

1. _____

2. _____

Special features:

1. _____

2. _____

www. mypurpose.de

A: Spontaneous evaluation

Ideas for the potential use of this profile:

_____

_____

_____

_____

_____

Ideas for the potential use of this profile:
(Continued):

_____

_____

_____

_____

_____

_____

_____

Step 5: Learning to recognize your problem-solving competence

As in Step 4, you should be open here to the spontaneous emergence of ideas. Over the coming days, be prepared to record anything that occurs to you – in writing! It is easy to forget to do this amidst the hectic pace of everyday life.

Then you should give these ideas, together with the information that you collect in the following period, time to mature. If it seems useful, repeat the whole process (from p. 131 onwards), so that you reach a new "GIVE" Integrity wheel and so that you ultimately can conduct a "considered evaluation (B)."

B: Considered evaluation

You need to be clear in your own mind which strengths, interests, and aptitudes you actually want to put into practice. In this phase you can expand your profile and no longer need to reduce it to two aspects. But do keep in mind the fundamental principle of this strategy: *strengthening strengths!*

List of strengths (talents, abilities, capabilities), interests, affinities, specific characteristics that I really want to apply – choose new options:

_____

_____

_____

_____

_____

_____

_____

_____

_____

_____

_____

_____

_____

_____

_____

_____

STOP

www. mypurpose.de

You first need to look again at the question of what and how you want to and are able to "give." Draw up a description of your particular competencies to solve problems and eliminate bottlenecks. It may be that you can immediately think of a particular problem or bottleneck, or even several, that you feel qualified to deal with. However, it is equally possible that you will need several days or a longer period before it becomes clear what your ideal field of activity, your mission, actually is. Be prepared to let the non-verbal part of your brain go to work here, in dreams and associations. Write down everything that occurs to you in the box (p. 151).

A particularly effective approach involves not only asking what sort of problems you are particularly suited to solving, but also asking what sort of bottleneck you feel particularly competent to eliminate. Bottlenecks are constellations in nature, from or between people, within or between organisations and businesses in which something essential is lacking, or there is a damaging surplus of one or more elements.

You should also resist the temptation to indulge in imaginative "escapes." It is highly probable that the greatest opportunities are to be found close at hand and, in most cases, precisely where you are right now. They are simply waiting for the necessary attentiveness to be discovered. Consider the farmer in South Africa who sold his thriving farm in order to devote himself to the search for diamonds when the first news of finds caused a wave of diamond fever. The search in ever-more distant regions depleted his assets to the point of bankruptcy. However, the person who purchased his farm almost immediately noticed unusual mineral fragments on his new property, which turned out to be precious stones that made him the wealthiest man of his time. Sometimes people behave like cows that crane their necks through a fence because they think there must be better pasture on the other side of the wire. The best chance of finding your own "diamond field" is in the environment with which you are already familiar – in your firm, your social surroundings, and among your customers and your suppliers.

**www.
mypurpose.de**

Description of tasks and problems or bottlenecks that I can deal with particularly well or would like to deal with:

_____

_____

_____

_____

_____

_____

_____

_____

_____

_____

_____

_____

_____

**www.
mypurpose.de**

Now identify the field of competence that promises you the most personal success, record it in the box on page 152. *And when you have reached this point, take a moment to congratulate yourself!*

STOP

Treat yourself to something nice – coming this far in integrating all the aspects of this process is something to celebrate!

My *most promising* task area (a problem or bottleneck, which I am particularly qualified to deal with):

_____

_____

_____

_____

_____

_____

_____

_____

_____

_____

_____

_____

_____

_____

_____

_____

_____

Step 6: Identifying your personal target group

This next step requires you to consider precisely where and/or for whom you can best apply your personal resources. You should always keep in mind that you are not alone with your goals but are surrounded by people who like you have very particular needs, wishes, and goals.

Given the strengths you have identified, think about how you can offer something useful to, or generate happiness for, other people, your clients or colleagues, your superior or boss, the owner of your company, or – remembering that you can also apply this working principle to the other five areas of life – your partner, your children, your parents, other relatives, your friends, or yourself (your mind, your body) in a way that corresponds to the needs and wishes of the respective "target group."

For whom, where, or how can I most *effectively* utilize my strengths? My personal target group:

_____

_____

_____

_____

_____

_____

_____

_____

"The sole meaning of life is to serve humanity."
LeoTolstoy

**www.
mypurpose.de**

Develop a specific, clear profile for your professional and private environment and familiarize yourself with it. When deciding how to apply your strengths, think of them as the missing piece in a puzzle. Selecting the right strategy means nothing more than applying your strengths at the correct, most effective point.

Phase 3: The complete Goal Scenario (HAVE and GIVE):

When you have completed this task, you can supplement the target scenario focusing on what you would like to have or achieve with the second part concerning what you are able and prepared to give. A goal developed on the basis of a value system in this way, which is also linked with your particular personality and uniqueness, can be realized to a quite different degree from goals suggested to you by others, or which you spontaneously seize upon when in a certain mood.

The second part of the Goal Scenario (see checklist for the first part p. 126)

When I state in the first part (see p. 126):
"I'm happy about the fact that I . . ."
(This is followed by a Goal Scenario – formulated in vivid and positive terms, including a date and using the present tense (and an active verb that expresses joy and enthusiasm) – that defines the goal in terms of quality and quantity, so that the moment when the goal is achieved can be precisely recognized.)
then, in the second part of the Goal Scenario, the corresponding statement is:
"I am achieving this by utilizing my strengths, which are . . .
(_____ **)**
(This is followed by a description of your particular strengths, i.e., your talents, abilities, and proficiencies.

Now you do not need to limit yourself to your six most pronounced strengths. You can include all the strengths that you are able and want to, in the relevant life areas. Strengths that you already have but do not want to utilize should be left out here.)

together with my interests

(_____)

(Here you need to decide which interest or interests you actually want to utilize in the relevant areas of your life. You need to decide, for example, whether you want to utilize an interest that you have perhaps pursued up till now only privately on a professional level, or whether you want to continue restricting this source of energy to your private life; whether you want to extend an interest that has only applied to your professional life to your sporting activities, etc.)

and utilize

(_____)

*(Here you need to describe your **special features**, insofar as you want or are able to utilize them in the relevant life area)*

in order to solve

(_____)

*(Here you need to list **tasks/problems/bottlenecks**, which you can see yourself solving)*

in relation to _____ ."

*(Here you need to describe **where, or in relation to whom**, you have identified a bottleneck – your personal target group, your target area. In the professional area, this might comprise problems in a business, in your department, with other market participants, clients, etc., or, in the health area, "lack of endurance" or "physical laziness," etc..*

Ecology check

Does my
Goal Scenario
fit to my life?
At this stage of the process – just to be sure you are on the right track – you should examine your Goal Scenario using an ecology check. This involves taking a comprehensive view of the possible changes to your life that result from realizing your Goal Scenario.

- Check that your goals are indeed your own. Have you perhaps been swayed by fashionable trends or other people to focus on activities that do not really mean a lot to you personally?

- Will the newly formulated Goal Scenario fit into your life? Examine all the essential people and activities in your life in order to ensure that the changes that ensue from your Goal Scenario will be completely positive. Is there any aspect that could trigger resistance? What is the positive intention behind this resistance?

How can you reformulate the Goal Scenario so that it is completely consistent for you?

Make a contract with yourself

Your goal formulation is a fixed contract with yourself and should, therefore, be provided with a place, date, and your signature. By doing this you are creating a bond between yourself and the goal.

However, the act of writing this down does not conclude the process. Now the transfer of the Goal Scenario into everyday life becomes decisive. To help you with this there is a secret recipe that is as old as it is effective, but which is not often actually used. The surest way to approach your goal is to adopt the habit of reading out the *Goal Scenario twice daily (if possible, aloud!)*.

If you have come this far with us, then we would like to heartily congratulate you. You can now be sure that you number among the 5% of the population who manage to make wishes become realities. Your attention is now focused, your energy is at a high level and directed, and you have decoded the secret of self-motivation for yourself.

No one can deprive you of this access to your own inner sources of strength. Moreover, you are free to fine-tune your motivational framework at any time or, if you wish, to completely restructure it. We promised at the outset not to lead you into a dependency on third parties who seek to motivate you, and for this reason, we have guarded against supplementing our text with motivational elements that you may already have encountered in other books in this field. Admittedly, the path we are suggesting is not an easy one to take; you have to take it alone and it demands a considerable investment of energy. However, for now you can be proud of yourself and, apart from the positive feeling you are enjoying anyway, you should give yourself an appropriate reward.

Before you launch into the second part of our book, take a look in the appendix at our reward list to see if you can find something that could lift your good mood even further – and treat yourself to it. You can surely allow yourself a little extrinsic motivation at this point!

And after so much "cool-headed" work, it is now time to bring some heart into the equation. It is important that you return to the text of your Goal Scenario and refine it so that it sounds inherently consistent to you when you read it out. It is like the work of an author: the written words need to trigger a fascinating internal image (or in the language of science: the verbal half of the brain must be linked with the visual, emotional half of the brain such that the two hemispheres are synchronized).

Live with a cool head and a passionate heart!

Since our intentions are emotionally enriched via the connections between the right half of the cerebrum and the limbic system beneath it, and the limbic system is, in turn, affected by resonance circuits of the vegetative nervous system, which are connected to our heart, we can assume that when we detect a positive feeling of coherence on reading our scenario we have in fact located our *"way of the heart."* Head and heart can thus establish an extraordinarily powerful and beneficial link, which will provide all the self-motivation you will need to realize your Goal Scenarios.

Regularity and continuity in your task are key here if you are to actually achieve something and not just dream of doing so. Endurance is the common factor that links all successful people, not intelligence, courage, or capital. A clear goal pursued with perseverance generates courage, stimulates the mind and can create realities.

Our life becomes meaningful when we take up challenges, the mastery of which enables us to cross personal borders.

The *"way of the heart"* is the way that makes sense for you. Things that make sense are things that correspond to your values. Clarity regarding your own value system is the precondition of every good decision, and only those who can make clear decisions can attain their goals.

Such an approach also provides a solid foundation for hundreds of moments in everyday life in which your brain must decide what should be processed, retained, and later remembered, and what is unimportant and can be immediately forgotten.

A person with clearly set goals automatically knows what is important.

"A big YES is required in order to be able to say this small no."
Stephen Covey

Without a clear goal we find ourselves doing too many things at the same time; we say yes at one time and no at another and achieve nothing. We cannot achieve everything and certainly not everything at the same time in our lives. We very often have to say NO when daily distractions promise us small pleasures, in order to preserve the time, energy, and concentration we need for the realization of the great dreams of our lives. As

Stephen Covey argues, *"A big YES is required in order to be able to say this small no."*

And we have seen that our life makes sense when we seek out challenges in the areas in which we can confirm our values. Clarity regarding our values system and its still unfulfilled aspects gives definition to our wishes, which we can then realize through the development of a Goal Scenario.

We have seen that combining this values aspect with the two-dimensional image of the flow channel creates a three-dimensional space. However, this model initially lacked a foundation, one which the process we have been engaging in enables us to identify and utilize. The stabie foundation of the space for FLOW experiences is the use of our talents and the development of our abilities. Our competence is constantly increased when we apply our talents and expand our abilities through constant learning. In Csikszentmihalyi's sense, this process results in a growth in our complexity, in our self, we realize our purpose of life.

To the extent that we are able to facilitate growth in our knowledge and abilities as well as our understanding of contexts, for instance, harmoniously link differentiation and integration with one another, we will generate flow experiences. Our lives will be characterized by a general feeling of achievement.

FLOW experience: the harmonious linking of differentiation and integration.

And if the knowledge that you are able to draw from available sources proves insufficient to meet the challenges you confront, then obviously, new knowledge is required. This also requires creativity, the aspect that completes our picture.

A lot of people use well-designed programs to improve their physical fitness. The system represented in the above diagram will enable you to improve your mental-emotional fitness, in other words, to train your mind: A healthy mind needs a healthy body – but a healthy body also requires a strong mind.

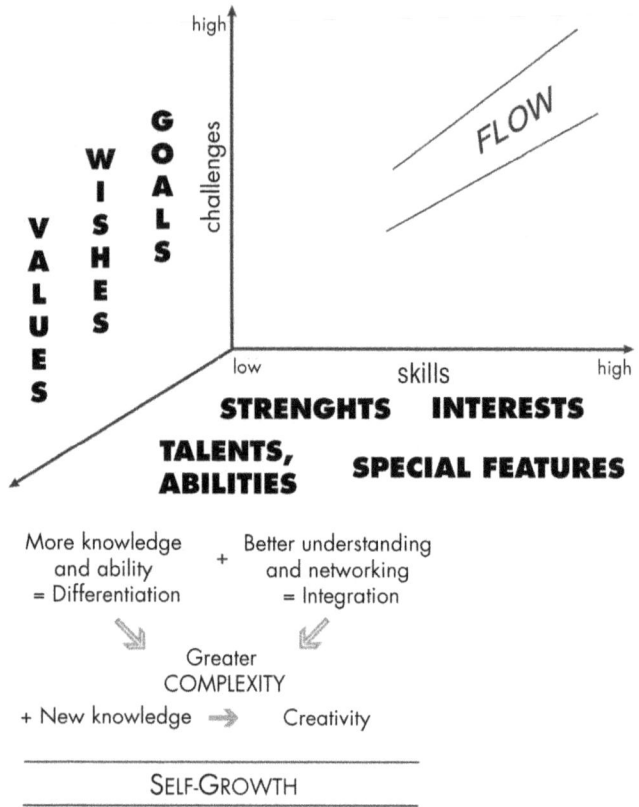

G **W**
O **I**
A **S**
V **L** **H**
A **S** **E**
L **S**
U
E
S

challenges

FLOW

low   skills   high

STRENGHTS   INTERESTS

**TALENTS,
ABILITIES   SPECIAL FEATURES**

More knowledge   Better understanding
and ability   +   and networking
= Differentiation   = Integration

And when
new knowledge is
required: mobilize
your creativity.

Greater
COMPLEXITY

+ New knowledge ⇒ Creativity

SELF-GROWTH

Figure 24: Growth of the self through the increase in complexity and the expansion of creativity

Phase 4: The art of "detached involvement" – letting go of your goals again

It may surprise you when we say that you now need to learn to let go of your goals again. This is not meant in any way to devalue what you have done up until now. As important as it is constantly to be aware of your goals and to pursue them, it is just as important to see these goals as a tool and not to become a tool of these goals yourself.

Do not link your personal identity and your sense of satisfaction with your life exclusively to the fulfillment of your goals. Avoid subjecting yourself completely to a self-generated pressure to achieve. Your goals are only markers that are there to provide orientation and direction for your life; they are not life itself. In part II we will deal in more detail with this idea – derived from the work of Jagdish Parikh – of "detached involvement" (see p. 178 ff.).

Check your goal contracts regularly

Furthermore, you should not see your goal formulations as something static and unchangeable. They are like life itself and can, indeed must, adapt to the process of your development and your life situation. On the basis of the constant change within and around us, we should constantly examine our goals with regard to their motivational power and relevance and, if necessary, reformulate them.

Read your Goal Scenario aloud twice a day

Once your subconscious has absorbed this goal, it will ensure that the task involved is fulfilled. On the one hand, it will make you receptive to information and stimuli that would otherwise rush by you unnoticed and, on the other, ensure that your ATTENTIVENESS and energy are not wasted on things that will distract you from pursuing your goal. Reading the Goal Scenario aloud twice daily will anchor it more deeply in your psyche and gradually transform it into an unconscious steering mechanism.

"Whatever the human mind can conceive, it can achieve."
(Napoleon Hill)

We have reached a point where it is appropriate to quote a very precise and motivating definition of the word *success*, as formulated by Earl Nightingale:

"Success is
the progressive
realization of a
worthy ideal."
Earl Nightingale

"Success is the progressive realization of a worthy ideal."

Everyone who has a goal that he or she continually pursues is successful – and this applies to every moment along the path they are traveling, not only to the achievement of the goal. This is the key to understanding the deeper meaning of the phrase, *"The way is the goal."*

If the feeling of success is confined to the very end of a process, when we actually achieve our goal, it is all too easy to lose control or, in the worst case, succumb to the driven fanaticism that can result from a fixation.

Now – right now, not later – take your diary and make a schedule for developing concrete objectives on the basis of these ideas. For each area of life you should reckon with one and a half to three hours in which you will be able to work completely alone and without interruption on your goal formulation.

(These time specifications relate to the first step. In the case of important goals, the time frame could double or even triple. However, you can be sure that you will probably never invest an hour of your life more productively than every hour you devote to this task! These hours will pay both value and interest at the same time.)

What happens next? – vision and purpose in life

The right way to plan learning and life consists of the art of small steps. It is important that you do not approach big tasks in the spirit of *"I'll only manage half of it anyway."* You need to divide big tasks into very small segments and then actually deal with them based on the principle of *"What I've set out to do will be completed."* Do not assume that writing out a Goal Scenario and reading it out twice daily will be sufficient. This is not a book of magic. You have given yourself a challenge and it will place demands on you. It may even be the case that parts of the route you have mapped out will prove extraordinarily difficult. In order to be able to take up these challenges, further preparation is required, along with a certain skill in dealing with obstacles (which incidentally do not have to come from outside but which you yourself are quite capable of creating).

You should, therefore, regard the following, second part of this book as accompanying you on the initial stretch of the path which you now have before you and supporting you in the realization of your project.

Before we proceed, a few thoughts that look beyond the immediate context and are designed to inspire you in the way you order your goals and deal with future scenarios for your life within the overall framework of a viable life perspective.

Vision and purpose in life: the source of personal charisma

Once you have had some experience with realizing short-term (a time frame of up to six months) and medium-term (six to 18 months) goals you will increasingly ask yourself what the connecting thread is. In what direction is the consolidation of my strengths, abilities, and particular features leading? *What makes me so unique? Why am I on this planet? What can I contribute to the world? – What is my mission?*

Anyone who has found the answers to these questions can increasingly structure their Goal Scenarios in the longer term and will be able to lead a calmer and happier life – in the face of all external challenges and tests of endurance. Goals involving challenges that can be realized by means of your specific, individual vocation, of course, constitute a very particular driving force. In such cases self-motivation grows out of the core of one's own personality.

"The apex of happiness is reached when the human being is prepared to be what he is."
Erasmus of Rotterdam

Long-term goals that are in harmony with a person's vocation can be described in terms of vision. A person with vision is someone who is able to reconcile long-term goals with his or her particular vocation. People who live in harmony with their vision, who lead lives in which their actual behavior is reconciled with their value system, radiate the appeal that we refer to as charisma.

How does charisma develop?

Life vision or "the idea of ourselves"

How often do we ask ourselves why our life is as it is? Many people experience their lives as a more or less meaningless collection of accidents. They feel as if they have been *"thrown"* into the world and left at the mercy of the twists and turns of fate. In order to give life structure and a level of meaning, we adopt values and goals from our surroundings, family, peer group, and society. This creates a level of security and strengthens our sense of community. However, in quieter moments or during crises we suddenly find it is no longer possible to avoid the question of whether we are really alive, whether we have a coherent identity, and whether the path we have taken in life is leading in a direction that will provide strength and confidence in the long term. If we study the life paths of significant, creative, and successful individuals, we will see again and again that these people have followed an inner vocation. This vocation can, in some cases, take shape as a clear vision in early childhood or – as is usually the case – as a vague idea that reveals itself piece by piece and, repeatedly overlaid by other ideas and images, takes years to find real expression. In the case of "late bloomers," this inner image does not reach the point at which it can be realized until they are 50, 60, or even 70 years old.

Amidst the stress and routine of daily life, many people never manage to pause and listen to this inner voice, never achieve the distance from their daily lives that is needed to discover, nourish, and strengthen their vision. And yet it is a clear vision, a strong sense of your unique, personal vocation that ensures that you will select those important, worthwhile challenges that correspond to your vocation. Mastering such challenges not only provides an intensive experience of happiness at the moment of success but also a deep sense of satisfaction when we look back later in life on what we have achieved.

The really interesting question is: where do these images of the future come from? Are we an empty page at birth that we can later write on and design as we wish, or is there already an idea within us of the person we will become? Is a visionary image already implanted within us that we "only" have to become aware of? If that is the case, then our task of achieving happiness in life consists in enabling this vision to unfold and making it clear and tangible.

This latter alternative is decisively advocated by the psychologist James Hillman, who writes, *"Just as the acorn contains all the information that is needed to grow a complete oak tree; so does the soul contain the entire history of a life, from the moment of birth to the end of a life."*

James Hillman

In such a view, the vision of life does not entail the realization of an arbitrarily constructed image but the realization of one's own inner core. The Romans referred to this as *"genius,"* the Indians describe this phenomenon using the concept of *"karma,"* and the Native Americans refer to it as *"dream spirit"* or *"mind spirit."*

The idea of the self

In Hillman's opinion, the life of Pablo Picasso provides support for this point of view. *"I am astounded at the way the word development is misused; I do not develop myself: I am."* Thus we can interpret his picture "le jeune peintre" (the young painter) as a portrayal of the acorn that has painted the oak.

"I do not develop: I am."
Pablo Picasso

However, it is not always the case that a clear image is present from the outset, one which then takes form with increasing nuances year by year. Sometimes this genius is concealed from us and eludes premature discovery in order to protect both itself and us. Charles Lindbergh, for instance, the man who completed the first solo flight across the Atlantic, reported that as a child he was mortally afraid of heights. Was it the very perception of this fear that defined his particular existential challenge, his determination to face the dangers of pioneering air travel, to deal with the risks of crashing, so that he could ultimately accept the risks with complete self-confidence?

It is often indirect and problematic initial signals – which we can only retrospectively interpret – that momentarily manifest a later vocation. Numerous other biographies provide support for Hillman's thesis.

Does the small Spanish boy hiding from the world behind his mother's apron have any notion that as a grown man he will courageously face wild bulls in the arena? At this point, the boy cannot respond to such an inner calling because he is not ready for the challenge of bullfighting. Courage and skill need to mature. He will need several years before he can follow a vocation as a bullfighter.

This *calling* is often manifested as an inner voice. This voice has its own particular features and it often takes a long time to learn to listen to it and then to interpret it correctly. In the case of Socrates, for example, this voice never said what he should do, but only what he shouldn't do. It was thus manifested as a warning, limiting voice.

"Sometimes, the genius seems to show only in symptoms and disorders, as a kind of preventive medicine, holding you back from a false route," as Hillman puts it.

This concept suggests that life paths are far from arbitrary and that each human life follows a particular path that makes sense for this person, and – if he or she listens to the call of the inner voice – generates a feeling of satisfaction with that life.

It is thus our task not only to grow into the future but also to locate our roots, to rediscover what constitutes our being instead of too often allowing ourselves to be influenced by outside ideas. The question is, as Castaneda's teacher puts it, *"Is it a way of the heart?"*

Late Bloomers: Looking back on a fulfilled life

The point at which this idea of one's life breaks through can vary radically. We know that Picasso's vision already manifested itself at the age of nine. In the case of bullfighters it is probably manifested around the age of 20. However, for many people this vision becomes clear at a later point in life. The phenomenon of the *"late bloomer,"* recognizing and living out their vocation beyond their 50th or 60th year, can often refer to people who, for a long time, have experienced life as meaningless and chaotic, and who gain an insight that enables them to retrospectively see their existence as rich and fulfilled.

Answering the questions posed at the beginning as to what you can be grateful for and what has already been achieved, combined with the engagement with your values system and the more intuitive process that follows on from it, can together provide indications of your *"idea of your self."*

And ask your best friend what he or she thinks you could be, or have always been, in terms of your inner essence. What frictions, conflicts, ruptures, or even breakdowns has your genius generated because it has (still) been unable to be what it wants?

Living visions – dead visions

It is important that you treat this idea gently and with a certain degree of sensitivity. Do not for example, form it as a rigid ideal. Obsessive images of your vision can also generate destructive ideals, which can then become a *"dead vision."* It would be as if an oak tree that has germinated on a steep slope and successfully resisted the trials of wind and weather were to be constantly angry because it *did not conform to the image* of an oak as an evenly growing tree in the middle of an oak forest.

Dead visions can hinder your growth.

Animals and plants do not have such thoughts; they simply live their "beingness." However, due to the difference between their vision and lived reality, human beings have the capacity to make their lives unnecessarily difficult and even to ruin them with destructive self-reproach.

The thought of your vision, the idea of your self, should make you feel enthusiastic and give you energy, not lead you into conflict and de-motivate you. You should therefore check if the quality of your vision gives you a feeling of power and makes you look forward to its fulfillment. If this is the case then it is a living vision. If it is not then it may be that the image is an unrealistic one that could ultimately hinder you and smother your energies.

A vision provides you with the orientation for your personal way of the heart.

Clarity concerning your own vision also helps you access the inner dynamic of the flow channel. You move in a vertical direction towards your vision of life and, by developing yourself along the horizontal axis and growing internally, you fulfill your calling, your mission. Your visions are your ideas of what you want to realize and achieve in life, and your mission consists of what you yourself are able to give to people and the world. When these two aspects are compatible, you will experience a feeling of authenticity, of being alive and of taking *the way of the heart.*

For instructions to this fantasy journey see page 67 onwards

Perhaps you have already been aware of the theme of your life for a long time, in which case these passages will, at best, confirm what you have already learnt from your own experience. However, in case you are still curious we suggest you try the following two exercises. They may help you come closer to your idea of yourself. In contrast to the first fantasy journey of a (or any) perfect day (see page 73 onwards) this fantasy moves five years into the future.

Guided fantasy journeys – imagining your vision

Exercise 1: "A day your own perception of yourself becomes clear." (based on Naomi Stephan)

Close your eyes and note how your breath becomes calm and regular. Breathe in deeply without effort and then let your breath escape calmly and gently.

Become aware of the movement of your chest and stomach.

Sense the pleasant heaviness of your body, how the earth's gravitation holds you softly and draws you more and more firmly to the ground.

Your arms are very heavy.

Your legs are very heavy.

Your torso is very heavy.

Draw your breath into the nape of your neck and your shoulders.

Your breathing and heartbeat are quite calm and regular.

Imagine now that you have just woken from a pleasant, deep sleep and it is now a day approximately five years in the future.

It is the day on which your own perception of yourself becomes clear – fantasy has become reality.

You get up and go slowly to the window of your bedroom.

Take a moment to look out the window and observe what there is to see.

Go through your morning routine of washing and dressing.

Then go through the door of your bedroom and down the stairs.

Pause briefly on the middle landing of the stairway and look at the old grandfather clock. Take note of the time before you go down the rest of the stairs.

You fetch the morning newspaper from the front door and feel quite curious because today there is an article in the paper about you.

You take the newspaper to the breakfast table and flick through the pages until you reach the section that has the article about you.

Take note of your feelings as you discover the article.

Have a look at the article and make a mental note of the headline.

Then look at the photo of you that is printed along with the article.

How are you dressed?

What is the expression on your face?

Are you sitting or standing?

Are you alone or pictured with other people?

Now read the article in your own time and notice your reaction to what you are reading.

What is the tone of the article?

Is it favorable or critical or objectively neutral?

What does it say about you?

What insights can you gain from the article in view of your own imagination of your future, your own conception of yourself or your mission in life?

You stay quite relaxed and peaceful. Your eyes remain closed. In your imagination, you now take a writing pad and pen and write down the first word that occurs to you, the word that describes your emotional reaction to the article you have just read.

You draw a line under this word and then write down three things that you will do today in connection with your own perception of yourself.

Put the pad down and come back again to the present.

Move and stretch yourself. Breathe a little deeper and open your eyes.

Now record in your book, what you would like to remember from your fantasy journey.

End of the fantasy journey.

Here are a few pointers as to how you can interpret what you have seen.

(Remember that what you have seen came from you yourself. Therefore, it represents personal information about you.) There is no right or wrong, no good or bad, only things that you have observed.

1. At which points did you have difficulty following the suggested imagery? When was it that you could not form any images at all?

2. What was the scene that you saw as you looked out your bedroom window?

3. What was the time when you went past the grandfather clock?

4. At that moment, did you feel relaxed, pressured by time, or even stressed?

5. What clothes were you wearing?

6. In which section of the newspaper was the article about you printed – under sports, culture, science, local news, business, or elsewhere?

7. What was the headline? What did the article contain?

8. Describe the photo.

9. What was your emotional reaction to the article?

10. What associations do you have with the words on your writing pad? What insights can you

gain regarding your perception of yourself, your future vision?

11. What other aspects of the experience occur to you.

What else would you like to remember with respect to your thoughts, bodily sensations, and your perception of yourself.

This fantasy journey addresses aspects such as:

Ask yourself: In which type of surroundings would I like to live? How would my home look? What would my living conditions be like in five years?

With what aspect of myself would I like to win the regard and recognition of my fellow human beings (what does it say in the article)?

How would I organize and arrange my ideal day-to-day existence.

Where would I live?

How would things need to be arranged so that I feel at my most happy and at ease?

What does this tell me about my own perception of myself, my mission in life, and my vision?

Perhaps you had some difficulty in imagining the article so clearly that you could read it. Maybe you did not even want to appear in the newspaper. If so, then do not concern yourself; just work as best you can with what comes to your mind.

This exercise is not dependent on the specific images that we put to you, but rather on the images, thoughts, and feelings that your fantasy journey released. All this is your material, and the ideas and notions that are occurring to you now are what are really important. But do not judge yet – they could include unrealistic or irrelevant images. Think of the onion: under a dry, brown skin is a soft, white interior; the dried-out exterior does not represent the essence of the onion. So it is with these fantasy journeys, too – of course, they will not correspond exactly with what will happen in the future. At best, they function as a stimulus for the imagination and as a supplier of new ideas. Use them as pure, raw material, not as a prognosis *(so as to be sure there is not misunderstanding.)*

The Creative Process

*The third dimension
of the creative process concerns the
deeper aspects of the human being.
Often this realm is thought of
as the domain of philosophy, metaphysics or religion.
But there is another lens through which to view this aspect
of human makeup, one without the limitations of beliefs,
dogma, creed, doctrine, or conviction. This lens explores
without an idea of what one might find.
This true exploration can open the door to the deepest source
of the creative process. For your life to be art, you cannot
ignore your own depth, your own reservoir of vitality.
Through the creative process, your true spirit and essence
is expressed throughout your life.
When you are in touch with this spirit,
you are transformed in many ways.
It impacts your life direction, your understanding of what's
important to you, and your quality of life.*

*It can be a platform from which to stand,
a touchstone for deepest values and highest aspirations,
a source of inner strength, and a fountainhead
for amazing intrinsic generative energy.*

'Your Life as Art' by Robert Fritz
www.robertfritz.co

PART II

Making Ideas Reality

Energy 1: Activating willpower – practicing composure

"We are dominated by everything with which our self becomes identified. We can dominate, direct and utilize everything from which we disidentify ourselves."

Roberto Assagioli

Self-motivation is one side of the coin; the other is developing the willpower required to make goal scenarios a reality. It is common for motivation and will to be confused with one another. Indeed both words are often regarded as having the same meaning and are used interchangeably. This is based on a fatal misunderstanding that we need to clear up here before proceeding. Motivation exclusively refers to motive power or driving force, the sources that move us to do something. However, to allow actions take their course, an additional focus is required – a bundling of our willpower.

The process of realizing a goal scenario and overcoming both external and internal obstacles also involves dealing with our "weaker self," which, in spite of whatever motivations are driving us, repeatedly attempts to play tricks on us and destroy our intentions.

"Happiness is another term for willpower."
Ralph Waldo Emerson

In his book *Act of Will*, Assagioli illustrates ways of utilizing one of the main functions of willpower: the regulation of psychological energies. He makes it clear that this does not involve the suppression of vital impulses. This regulation is based on becoming aware of the efficacy of these forces, and achieving clarity and stability in those areas where willpower is weak or is dominated by other biological or psychological energies. This, in turn, lays the groundwork for greater self-confidence, satisfaction, and happiness.

"Three phases of development of will: Recognition that will exists – Realization of having a will – Being a will."
Roberto Assagioli

Here, too, the keyword is attention. ATTENTION is the key to concentration, and concentration consolidates willpower.

Images or mental conceptions have the tendency to generate corresponding physical states and external actions.

"The clear and constant maintenance of conceptions of action," writes Assagioli, *"leads to a deliberate use of the motor potential inherent in the images and ideas, which is expressed in the psychological law: images or mental conceptions have the tendency to generate corresponding physical states and external actions."*

Yet although Assagioli emphasizes the necessity of training concentration and attention (and offers a wide range of exercises for this purpose), he also makes clear that the exercise of willpower must never be allowed to lead to fixation, to an unexplained identification with a goal.

As well as instead of either-or

At first glance, this may seem somewhat paradoxical and foreign to the traditions of Western thought, which is influenced by the Aristotelian notion of "either-or."

So, on the one hand, we have a dated and signed contract with ourselves together with the concentration, attention, and commitment to reach the goal we have set. On the other hand, we have a warning against fixation, against rigid identification. How are these two aspects compatible?

Letting go and trusting in your own path

Eastern cultures tend to find it easier than our own to think and live within contradiction, and one Indian author, Jagdish Parikh, has endeavored to bridge these two cultural tendencies with his concept of *"management by detached involvement."* In our Western tradition we can refer to the thought of Heraclitus, who saw, behind all contradictions, the effect of a *"hidden harmony."* No day without night, no love without hate, no winter without summer … This concept can also be applied to the apparent contradiction between consciously pursuing a goal while also being able to "let go." Put simply, it involves developing trust in our own path.

Jagdish Parikh proposes that we should regard our different roles in life with all their contradictions as a "life game," as a sport that we can pursue externally with all the internal concentration required of a good player or sportsman. This enables us to come to terms with all the changes and transformations which life brings us and which we have no influence over. There are, of course, forces that are stronger than our will, but without a strong will we are unable to take advantage of what Rollo May describes as the scope between *"freedom and destiny."*

"Living:
Utilizing the scope
between freedom
and destiny."
Rollo May

We need to recognize, above all, that along with rational considerations, there is a range of irrational forces that massively influence our inner processes and that can exercise control over our external behavior. Freedom of choice (a notion that is, in fact, contested by a number of leading brain researchers) can only earn its name if we are able to uncouple our will from genetic, biological, and social forces that colonize us and dominate us in the form of idealized roles, fears, hopes, and desires.

The contradictory state of detached involvement becomes bearable once we have achieved an inner composure on the basis of the knowledge – or, more accurately expressed, the experience – that we are only really able to reach a goal if we first let go of it. The logical nature of the rules governing language means that it is difficult to describe the internal process this implies. One needs to have actually experienced it in order to comprehend it. Therefore, our aim here is more to provide an explanation of what you will feel when you have achieved this state than to make a direct contribution to your achieving it.

Having said this, we would like to offer you an exercise that is suggested by Assagioli as a way of increasing inner composure.

This guided meditation is based on the idea of "identification with the conscious self." It is designed, primarily, to help release us from preoccupations with certain aspects of our self, which divert us from our goals and cause us to sink into inertia. This release is achieved through letting go of the identification with old ideas, by gaining an inner distance.

Letting go of the
identification with
aspects of your
life is an impor-
tant step towards
freedom!

The serene distance towards various aspects of your life is an important step toward the freedom to act in different ways in every situation. Human life is subject to permanent change. This means that we are constantly compelled to abandon particular structures and certainties, and thus, the identifications that are an expression of these structures. This allows for a creative reorganization in order to master changing demands coming from our external environment and to realize new wishes generated internally.

Every identification with an individual aspect of your existence (e.g. the fixation on physical attractiveness, the idea of being able to "freeze" an emotional connection forever, the assertion of an idea or an ideological claim) or the identification with a role ("employer," "father," etc.) can result in grief and disappointment if you attempt to cling to, or resuscitate, "the good old days." By contrast, you can progressively learn to link the different parts and aspects of your personality into a comprehensive synthesis and to be open to life.

The more successful you are with letting go of the associations, the freer you will be from the oppressive claims of the primary system of drives, and the more effectively the "self" motivation of the secondary system of drives will be able to shrug off the "weaker self." It is only when we overcome these identifications with the "archaic" parts of our personality that we can develop the willpower required to reach our goals, to realize our values.

However, letting go of the identification does not entail that de-identification blocks or represses our feelings. Quite the opposite: Even if our feelings, even if they are pleasant but create unpleasant effects, we can learn to understand them as powerful indicators. Feelings are information; they represent possibilities of learning more about ourselves and others.

As Stephen Covey puts it, *"It is about gaining a moment of attentive awareness between the feeling and the possible reaction in terms of action. In such moments we have the chance to increase the quality of our lives."* We can then decide whether we want to identify or de-identify with a particular aspect of a particular situation.

If possible, establish a fixed time during the day when you can meditate, and choose a quiet place where you can be completely undisturbed for 15 minutes. Sit comfortably on a chair, keeping your back straight and without touching the backrest. Register the thoughts and feelings that arise and then let them go. Now return to the object of meditation, your mental focus (which you yourself decide on – see the following steps).

Self-identification exercise – based on the work of Roberto Assagioli

Read or, even better, speak the following passages. While doing it, make yourself comfortable and relaxed.

Letting go of the identification with the physical aspect of cognition

I now become conscious of the existence of something that is my body, but this body is not me. I am not my body. That entity which I am, which I call my self, exists but it is not the same as my body. My body has an identity and I myself have my own distinct identity. Both are related: when my physical body is healthy, I notice this just as I notice when it is sick. I realize that, at certain times, it is tired; at other times it is fresh and lively. But I am not my body; I possess another, quite distinguishable identity. I feel the tiredness, but I am not the tiredness.
(Cast you mind back now to an occasion when you really felt this separation of mind and body. Perhaps you are at a party, feeling flat; the drinks are warm, the music listless, and the people boring. You feel out of place and become aware of a great tiredness. It overcomes you. You want just one thing: to go home to your bed and sleep. You say goodbye and then, at the moment you are about to

leave, another guest arrives who greets you warmly. At that instant you think to yourself: "What an enchanting person!" You stay for a nightcap; ten minutes later you are dancing and it is not until five hours later that you feel the first signs of tiredness. Haven't you have experienced this or something similar before?)

The varying states of my body are discernible to me; I observe that I have a body; but my real self, my ego is something different. Sometimes, I think that I am my body; on some occasions, I am my body absolutely. But now, for the purpose of this exercise, I will rid myself of this idea. For a certain period of time that I myself will determine, I will no longer identify my self with my body. I will marvel at my body as a miracle – a precious tool of experience and activity in the outer world – but it is only that, a tool. I will look after it, keep it in good health, remembering that it is not me.

For the next minute, close now your eyes and repeat the following sentence to yourself:

"I have a body but my body is different from what I am myself."

Gradually understand with ever-increasing certainty that this statement is true and that it represents an empirical fact that you yourself can truly comprehend.

Open your eyes again and continue on with the following exercise in which it will become clear that you and your feelings are not one and the same.

Letting go of the identification with the emotional aspect of cognition

It is clear to me now that I have feelings, but I am not the same as my feelings. My feelings change, often for reasons I understand, but sometimes not. Feelings come and

*go – they cause my heart to swell; they scare me some-
times. They can change from love to hate, from calmness
to anger, from joy to grief; but my own identity remains
unaffected. My feelings cannot change my true nature,
the essence of my self does not change. "I am who I am."
I myself am not as variable as my moods. Anger goes
away eventually just as luck comes and goes; thus, I
know I myself am neither my anger nor my luck. I can
watch my feelings and often understand them. I can even
learn, gradually, how to direct my feelings, to use them
and integrate them with my self. But it is clear that my
feelings do not define me.*

At this point, you might like to try de-identifying
with particular feelings that sometimes seize control of you completely. It should become clear to
you that, though you may be experiencing rage,
you are not the rage itself. Or you can de-identify
with particular personality traits, unwanted desires,
dependencies, supposed necessities, etc. In this
way, you can place your self and your feelings
apart, without having to suppress or deny them.
The feelings are there, but you are not the same
thing as your feelings.

For the next minute, close your eyes and repeat the
following sentence over and over.

**"I have feelings, but my feelings are different from
what I am myself."**

Gradually understand with ever-increasing certainty that this statement is true and that it represents
an empirical fact that you yourself can truly comprehend.

Open your eyes again and continue on with the following exercise in which it will become clear to you
that you and your thoughts are not one and the
same.

Letting go of the identification with the mental aspect of cognition

When I think, I use my intellect, but I am not my intellect. I use my intellect to perceive the world and people, but I myself am not my intellect. I employ my intellect as a valuable tool of discovery and expression, but it does not represent the essence of me. I realize that I am constantly developing new thoughts, gaining new knowledge (which sometimes I forget again), gathering new experiences (sometimes important, sometimes not), and creating new ideas that can astound me. But sometimes, my intellect refuses to obey me. Therefore, it cannot be all that is me. It gives me the ability to perceive both my outer and inner world, but it is not me myself. Consequently, I am aware that: "I have an intellect, but I am not my intellect. I can think, but I am not my thoughts."

For the next minute, close your eyes and repeat the following sentence over and over.

"I have a mind, but what I am is different from my mind. I can think but my identity is different from my thoughts."

Gradually understand with ever-increasing certainty that this statement is true and that it represents an empirical fact that you yourself can truly comprehend.

Open your eyes again and continue on with the following exercise. It will become clear to you that after disassociation from your body, feelings, and thoughts, that which remains is the nucleus of yourself.

Identification of your conscious self

What am I then? What remains when I have rid myself of the associations with my body, feelings and thoughts?

It is the essence of my self – a nucleus of pure self-consciousness. That is the enduring facet – the continuum in the ever-changing flow of my daily life. It is here I find my own identity, the sensation of what it is to be me; that constitutes my life force, my being, my inner harmony.

I recognize and acknowledge my self as a center of pure self-awareness and creative dynamic energy. I know that from this center of true identity, I can learn how to observe, control, and harmonize my psychological processes and physical body. Even in the midst of my daily life, I want to achieve a steadfast awareness of this fact and use it, so that this elevated plane of consciousness can help me, and give my life a greater significance and direction. It is this center that gives my will its strength, constancy, and stamina.

For the next minute, close your eyes and repeat the following sentence over and over.

"I recognize and reaffirm with complete composure that my own identity is free and can only be brought to expression by me myself. I am, and remain, a powerful nucleus of will and attentiveness."

Gradually understand with ever-increasing certainty that this statement is true and that it represents an empirical fact that you yourself can truly comprehend.

Conclusion of exercise

Remain for a while in this state and then return by counting backwards from ten to one, becoming more awake with each number. Take a deep breath and stretch your limbs. Open your eyes and quickly flex your forearms ten times and stretch.

What does regular (if possible, daily) practice give us? Roberto Assagioli again:

"If ATTENTION is increasingly focused on the state of consciousness, through this stage of distancing yourself from the identification can be shortened. The aim is to develop enough skill through this practice to be able to get through this stage of distancing yourself from the identification quickly and dynamically, and then to remain in "I" consciousness as long as one wishes. One can then – at will and at any moment – de-identify with every overwhelming feeling, every annoying thought, every inappropriate role, etc., and gain a clear understanding of the situation, its meaning, its causes, and the most effective form of action from the point of view of the removed observer."

This clarification exercise is, however, only one aspect of training the will. A second aspect consists in accepting that in its early developmental phases, the will is a very weak force. In such phases we find it all too easy to let the "comfortable" sides of our own natures dominate us. As Assagioli writes: "One grants internal impulses or external influences control of one's personality."

He continues, "This behavior could be described as a refusal to pay the price demanded by a worthwhile undertaking. This often also applies to the development of the will; yet one cannot reasonably expect that the will can be trained without the investment of effort and repeated practice that is required for the successful development of other qualities of a physical or intellectual nature. Such an effort is more than worthwhile because the use of the will is the basis of every activity. Highly developed willpower will, therefore, increase the effectiveness of all future endeavors."

Energy 2: Overcoming external obstacles

"Master one difficulty and you will hold 100 others at bay."
Confucius

It would be unrealistic to assume that goal scenarios realize themselves, even though this can seem to be the case. It is better to proceed from the assumption that you will have to face obstacles before reaching your goal. Dealing with such obstacles is the acid test for your self-motivation. Surprises are always a possibility, but it is how we deal with them that is decisive. The least that we can do is optimally prepare ourselves for the realization of our goals, in other words, give ourselves the time to reflect and plan, and to develop original ideas. This chapter deals with how we can overcome external obstacles that stand in the way of the realization of the goal scenario.

"Things of beauty can even be made from the stones laid in our path."
Johann Wolfgang von Goethe

An even greater difficulty is posed by the obstacles that we generate: the traps that we set for ourselves. In such cases, fundamental assumptions and internal dogmas play a large and often fateful role. We will deal with such internal obstacles in the next chapter, "Energy 3: Dissolving Emotional Blockades" (see p. 203 ff.).

The realization of a goal scenario

1. Clarification: task or problem?

Our point of departure is the desire or necessity to move from a given situation (IS) to an envisioned or proposed real future situation (SHOULD), which is distinguished from the IS situation to such a pronounced and positive degree that the achievement of the SHOULD situation justifies the required effort.

The question that needs to be answered with regard the realization of a goal scenario is: how do I move from the IS situation to the SHOULD situation? The first phase involves simply thinking – in the sense of mentally rehearsing forms of action.

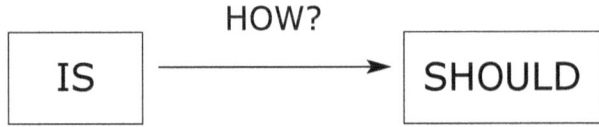

The SHOULD situation needs to be described as clearly as possible (in terms of both quantity and quality – see "Goal Scenario"). What you require here, above all, is a significant investment of imagination. You need to think about what the situation will look like shortly before the realization of the goal (the final stage of the realization process). Then you need to use your imagination to envision the situation prior to this, then the one before that, and so on, until you reach your point of departure, which corresponds to the present IS situation. This method of thinking backwards helps to develop your focus on the respective stages. If you track the process from the beginning, step by step into the future, there is a danger that you will become lost in a vast array of variations and, as a consequence, stop thinking and simply begin to act.

Why planning step by step into the future usually fails.

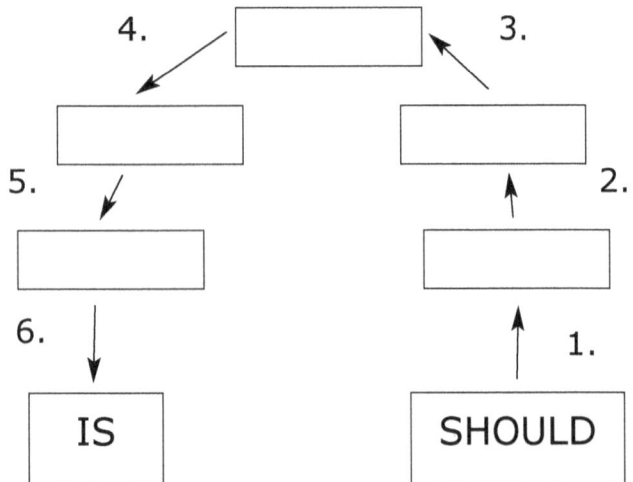

Only now, in the second phase, should you think step by step, from the initial situation through to the SHOULD situation, and check whether you have over-looked anything, whether you need to elaborate some aspects or introduce new ones, whether you need to consider alternatives, and whether you should aban-don certain elements that do not make sense in the pres-ent context.

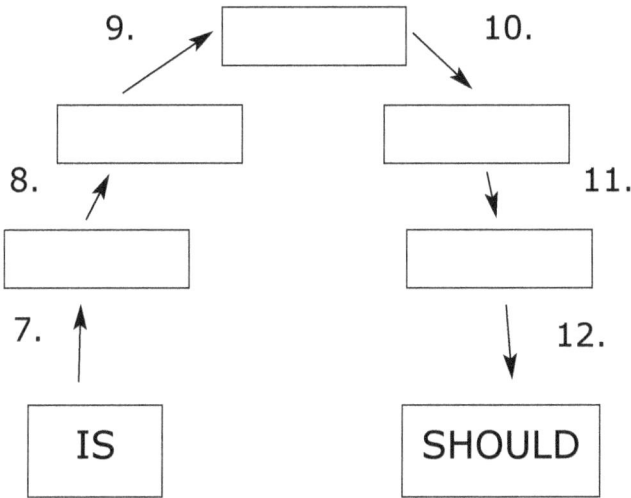

9.   10.

8.   11.

7.   12.

IS   SHOULD

Depending on whether the

          – activities

          – needed resources

          – persons

          – information

required for this process are

     known   or   **unknown**

you are dealing with either

     a task   or   **a problem.**

"A wrong answer is
easily identified,
but it takes
originality to detect
a wrong question."
Antony Jay

This is an important difference, as you will soon see. This is where the experts are separated from the amateurs. Experts do not make avoidable mistakes, and equating tasks with problems would be a mistake.

Have you ever
thought about
the difference
between tasks
and problems?

Tasks	Problems
are solved through deliberation, referring back to previous experiences (our own or others'), following rules, using proven methods, techniques, know-how, etc. Learning to solve tasks is something we learn through professional training and in the context of our professional lives, and it will, therefore, not be discussed in great detail here.	Before we speak of a "problem" we should be sure that the desired result cannot be reached by any known means. If, despite all our efforts to think through the issue, analyzes, and research, we are still unable to identify individual, many, or even all steps from the IS to the SHOULD situation, then we are dealing with a problem. It is typical of problems that they cannot be solved in this way – at least not initially. They require us to find something new, to think creatively.
However, it should be noted that it is very important to check carefully whether we are facing a task in a given situation. Compared with problems, tasks require significantly less effort and offer significantly greater prospects of success (= a significantly lower risk).	This, of course, also applies when it is clear from the outset that we need a new, original solution, when finding something "new" constitutes the problem itself.

2. Solving problems and creative thinking

When dealing with genuine problems we must move away from what we know, break rules, ignore know-how, embrace contradictions, and think illogically, laterally, and in terms of contradiction and paradox. What is needed is creative thinking. And we must keep in mind that our goal is to make a problem solvable, to allow it to become a solvable task.

Paul Watzlawick (in his book *Solutions*, written with John H. Weakland and Richard Fisch) distinguishes between the different approaches in terms of first-order solutions (= tasks) and second-order solutions (= problems).

First-degree solutions and second-degree solutions

Watzlawick introduces his book with a story that makes this distinction very clear:

"When in 1334 the Duchess of Tyrol, Margareta Maultasch, encircled the castle of Hochosterwitz in the province of Carinthia, she knew only too well that the fortress, situated on an incredibly steep rock rising high above the valley floor, was impregnable to direct attack and would yield only to a long siege. In due course, the situation of the defenders became critical: they were down to their last ox and had only two bags of barley corn left. Margareta's situation was becoming equally pressing, albeit for different reasons: her troops were beginning to be unruly, there seemed to be no end to the siege in sight, and she had similarly urgent military business elsewhere. At this point the commandant of the castle decided on a desperate course of action, which to his men must have seemed sheer folly: he had the last ox slaughtered, had its abdominal cavity filled with the remaining barley, and ordered the carcass thrown down the steep cliff onto a meadow in front of the enemy camp. Upon receiving this scornful message from above, the discouraged duchess abandoned the siege and moved on. The castle was saved."

A crazy and dangerous idea provided the way out of a desperate situation.

Using a range of similar examples, Watzlawick and his co-authors clearly show that processes of change very often take place very suddenly and, equally, are often based on illogical, paradoxical notions. Your own experience no doubt confirms this.

Particularly interesting in this context is the fact that the authors have analyzed why this is the case and present a series of conclusions that can be utilized in quite concrete ways when dealing with everyday tasks. Their decisive finding is that there are two types of change:

The first type occurs within a particular system that remains unchanged, whereas the second changes *the system itself.*

Take the example of a nightmare. Within the dream we can try what we like – running away, hiding, fighting back, jumping out the window. Yet we all know that changing from one of these behaviors to another does not lead to the resolution of the nightmare. We can't shake our pursuers off. The solution lies in changing from the dream to the waking state. However, the waking state is not part of the system of the dream, but a change to a completely different system, one of alert consciousness. It is a transition to a quite different state. Since there is no ready terminology for these different processes of change, the authors speak of a first-order change when dealing with the change from an internal state to another within an invariant system. An example of this is the possibility of changing speed within a defined gear by giving more or less gas.

Second-order change
A second-order transformation or change occurs when the system itself undergoes a change (such as when, using the same example, changing gears allows the driver to use a quite different speed range.)

Aristotle categorically ruled out such changes on the grounds that " ... *there cannot be motion of motion, or becoming of becoming or in general change of change.*" His antipode Heraclitus already saw things differently in that he argued that it was impossible to step into the same river twice and concluded, "*All change is contradictory; therefore, contradiction is the very essence of reality.*" Prior described the development of the concept of change as follows: "*It would hardly be too much to say that modern science began when people became accustomed to the idea of change, e.g. to the idea of acceleration as opposed to simple motion.*"

Using an analogy to mathematical group theory on the one hand, and logical type theory or set theory on the other, the authors make clear how efforts to change within a group with first-order changes can only lead to more of the same – thereby possibly increasing rather than decreasing the problem.

Changes within a group must be introduced from outside, from a meta level, and are, therefore, by definition second-order changes. And since these second-order changes are completely separate from the first-order structure, they necessarily seem to be as illogical and paradoxical as the decision by the commandant of the castle of Hochosterwitz to throw away his last food to avoid starvation.

However, differentiating between the two processes of change can be very difficult in practice. And when we

Changing the intervention level:

The problem cannot be solved within the frame of reference in which it has been created, but only at a higher level outside the original system.

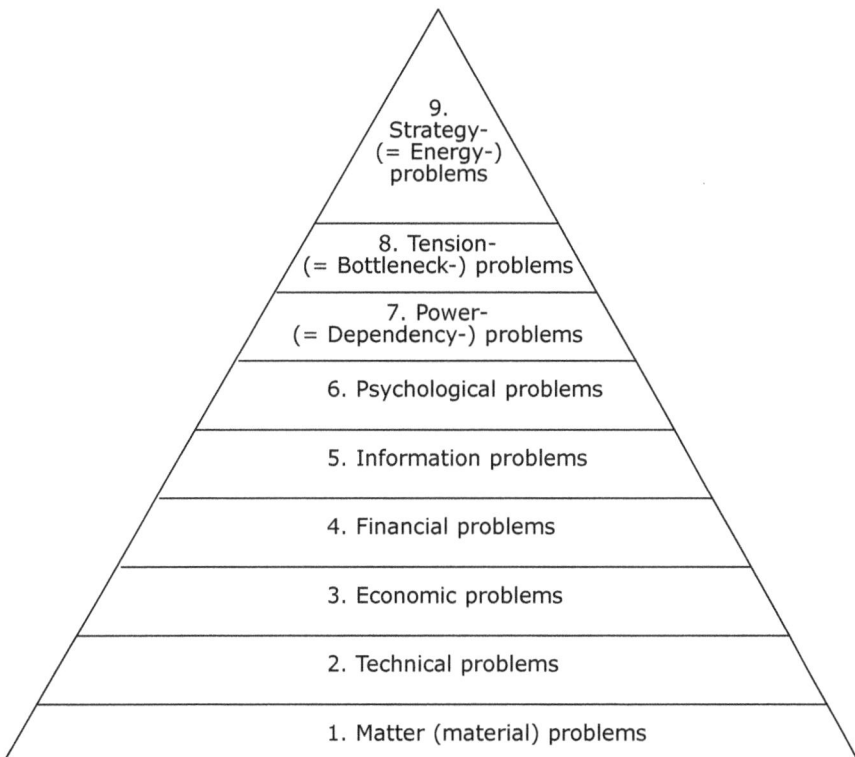

9.
Strategy-
(= Energy-)
problems

8. Tension-
(= Bottleneck-) problems

7. Power-
(= Dependency-) problems

6. Psychological problems

5. Information problems

4. Financial problems

3. Economic problems

2. Technical problems

1. Matter (material) problems

Figure 25: Problem levels: first- and second-order solutions (based on Mewes/Watzlawick).

do not take this difference into account and confuse the two processes, we can find ourselves attempting to realize solutions that not only fail to lead to the desired change but make the problem involved completely insoluble.

The following pyramid diagram illustrates different problem levels.

If a problem cannot be solved at the level that has generated it, then it can be useful to try a solution from a higher level.

Example: Reducing oil production to stabilize and/or increase the oil price in autumn/winter 1973–74.

Original problem level: "1. Material problems" (crude oil scarcity)

First-order solution (= at the first level): In the West new oil wells were drilled and new oil fields were looked for. Petrol and heating oil prices were increased. Energy-saving measures were introduced.

Second-order solutions:

2. "Technical" level:

Development of far more economical combustion engines and new heating burners, better housing insulation, development of new sources of energy (solar energy, heat pumps, etc.)

4. "Financial" level:

Price increases, taxation reductions coupled with energy-saving measures

5. "Information" level:

Detailed consumer information on the finite nature of fossil fuels

6. "Psychological" level:

Strong psychological influence through the ban on Sunday driving

3. Excursus: The beginning of scientific research into creativity

How do such leaps, original notions, ideas, and creative solutions come about? Over the centuries, different agencies have been seen as responsible for creativity – in ancient Greece the Muses and in Christian culture God. It was only toward the end of the 19th century that the actual process of the development of ideas became a subject of scientific reflection. In 1926, following on from early work by Helmholtz and Poincaré, Graham Wallas published his groundbreaking work on creative thinking *The Art of Thought*. Wallas describes the process-character of idea generation and divides this process into phases that follow on from one another, although they take quite different periods of time. In his book *Creativity and Innovation*, John W. Haefele uses this insight to formulate a highly practical approach to everyday life. Then, in 1976, Silvano Arieti published *Creativity – the Magic Synthesis*, a work based on studies of the literature in this area and empirical observations. At almost the same time, the first publications appeared that introduced a quite new phase of research within this extensive field. Brain researchers such as Roger Sperry, Michael S. Gazzaniga, Joseph E. and Glenda M. Bogen, Klaus Hoppe, and many others introduced the asymmetries of the two hemispheres of the cerebrum as a factor into the discussion of creativity.

The four phases of the creative or problem-solving process (based on Wallas):

I. Preparation, definition of issue, problem formulation, basic idea

Search for solution, collecting material, structuring problem analytically, review of proven solutions, technical know-how, logical reflection, Internet research, internal/external databases, morphological boxes, etc.

Scientific
creativity research

The four phases
of the creative
process

II. Incubation time

III. Brain wave, idea, illumination

IV. Implementation, realization

Comparison with Phase 1, reality check, adaptation, revision – if required, repetition of the process from Phase I

4. The practical realization of the problem-solving process

Practical implementation of the problem-solving process

Phase I of the creative process: task definition, IS/SHOULD analysis, initial attempts at a solution

The literature agrees: 50% of a problem is solved if the target solution is precisely defined in language.

Penetrating and formulating the problem, envisaging the target, general problem identification, emotional connection, analysis of initial situation (causes and background), analysis of the desired SHOULD situation.

A: IS analysis:

1. What are the individual elements of the initial situation?

2. What are the relationships between the elements?

3. What causes and developments have led to this situation?

4. Motive or reason for change? What reasons are there for changing this situation?

B: SHOULD analysis:

1. What do I actually want? (Examination of correspondence with the value to be realized. If relevant: What does my client actually want) Question: What goal should be reached?

2. What is important to me (if relevant, to my client)? (Setting priorities within what is possibly an extensive goal-setting process.)

3. What uses should the solution offer for whom?

(This key question must be answered in detail. Even if time is limited and there are not enough resources available for an extensive analysis, it is, nevertheless, important that the answer to this question is formulated in written form!)

4. What related conditions must the solution fulfil? (Time frame, financial budget, legal requirements, internal regulations, etc.)

5. What are the consequences of the achievement of the goal? (For me, for those involved, for those not involved, for the world, ecological consequences, etc.)

This analysis can lead to a new, modified task definition. In cases where solutions are being sought for a third party it is absolutely necessary that the client is given a status report.

After – and sometimes already during – the analysis phase, the search for approaches to a solution can begin:

Collection of information, data, facts
(objective material)

Generation of solution approaches
(subjective material)

Organization of ideas

Phase II of the creative process: Incubation

"Hatching plans" with the collected material
Allowing the solution to "mature"
"Incubation" of the solution
"Letting it work within you"

Due to the particular psychological components of the incubation phase (anxiety, frustration, feelings of inferiority, impression of personal incompetence extending to extreme tension and postponement, avoidance, escape strategies – e.g. producing another problem, passing the buck, denial, etc.) many people give up during this phase.

By contrast, creative people exhibit frustration, tolerance, patience, endurance, continuous variation between intense effort and completely letting go, an ability to "switch off" and to delegate problem-solving to the unconscious (or, to use another metaphor, "the nonverbal hemisphere").

Numerous creative techniques have been developed to shorten the incubation phase and to improve the quality of solutions. Apart from *Zwicky's Morphological Box* approach, which can already be applied in the first phase of the creative process, these methods serve to intensify the activities of the nonverbal hemisphere, to reduce disturbances by the linguistic function, and, **above all, to improve communication between the two hemispheres.** At the same time, they promote cooperation between the front and back areas of the brain by overcoming fear blockages, perception filters, and divergences between stored experiences, and generate new and necessary viewpoints. The secret of creativity is far from being revealed, but we now know something more about the circumstances that tend to facilitate it. Recommended methods include:

Brainstorming
6 – 3 – 5 ("written brainstorming")
Synectics
Free association

Mind mapping
Progressive abstraction
Osborn's checklist
etc.

It is definitely useful to develop a friendly relationship with the visual, emotional, sensory, synthesizing, and holistic hemisphere. Creativity is not a singular, methodical act, but a question of consciousness, of internal focus, and of the way the imagination, the irrational, the illogical, fear, and enthusiasm are dealt with at a personal level. It has to do with the preparedness to set goals, but also with the preparedness to play with ideas. Finally, human creativity is very often (perhaps even always) a question of the heart, of love, of devotion.

Phase III of the creative process: idea generation, flashes of inspiration, insight, solution

Suddenly – and usually surprisingly – our spirits lift. Accompanied by a joyful, clear, flowing feeling, we become aware of the solution, the idea comes, a flash of inspiration sparks through the brain. The new idea sometimes emerges in small steps that follow one after the other, sometimes in a single moment. This almost always happens when we are not concentrating intensively on the solution – although this can certainly also happen – but incidentally, when we are engaged in other activities (e.g. while walking, showering, driving a car, playing sport, listening to music, or at night while dreaming, etc.) However, given a certain amount of training and the development of a certain level of skill, insights can emerge quite directly as the result of targeted efforts.

Have you ever been surprised by your own ingenuity while in the shower?

Phase IV of the creative process: realization, application, elaboration

Many ideas need to be worked on. They have to be checked in terms of their realistic and unrealistic aspects. The necessary measures, means, time, and, in some cases, other people must be defined as precisely as possible and, in the context of implementation, repeatedly adapted to prevailing realities and developments (planning process). It is also necessary to check that the ideas for the solution(s) correspond to the task definition. In the case of alternative solutions a process of decision-making is required.

The following criteria can be helpful in this decision-making process:

(Important! Maintain the order presented here!)

5. The decision-making process:

And if you have too many ideas:

Here, you can find the best way out of the problem.

This checklist for the decision-making process can also be downloaded from the Internet.

www. mypurpose.de

a) Solution concepts **must be able to actually achieve** the goal. Solution concepts that cannot achieve the goal need to be discarded (but only here – not at the moment when they first emerge!!).

b) The **means** that are required must be directly **available** or realistically attainable in the foreseeable future.

If necessary – where the necessary means for all solution concepts are equally absent – Phases I–III of the creative process should be repeated.

c) The solution must specify the attainment of the goal not only in terms of material but also time. Solution concepts that do not lie within the framework of goal attainment should be discarded.

d) Establish **with what degree** of certainty the remaining solution concepts will reach the targeted goal. The solution concept that offers the greatest certainty of reaching the goal is the solution.

e) The means should realize the goal as **completely** as possible. The solution concept that offers the highest degree of **goal attainment** is the best solution to the problem.

Often the best solution results from the combination of several elements of different ideas.

Once the decision has been made the stage is set for:

Action

"There is nothing good – except if you do it!"
Erich Kästner

After a certain time: check and evaluate the results ("Accumulating experiences ...").

Your Life as Art

You can create your life in the same way an artist develops a work of art.

When you begin to approach your life from that orientation, you transform your world. You become more directly involved in your own life building process, you create more of what you truly want, and you broaden the quality of your life experience.

You can conceive of the life you want to bring into being as an artist conceives of a painting, take strategic actions to build such a life as the artist takes all the necessary actions to create the painting, and inhabit the life you want to create as the artist may hang the painting on the wall to experience it.

Expressed another way, you can be the playwright, and also the lead actor, and also the audience for your own life play.

You can be your work, and you can be its author. And, like the artist, writer, playwright, filmmaker and composer, the creative process can be your operational practice.

From 'Your Life as Art' by Robert Fritz

(www.robertfritz.com)

Energy 3: Dissolving emotional blockages

"The life of a person is what his thoughts make of it."
Marc Aurel

It is extremely important (in spite of all one's commit-ment to pursuing a self-defined goal until it is actually reached) to maintain the inner flexibility that allows you to choose paths different to those you originally plan-ned, and – because the goal is unrealistic or becomes unachievable due to unforeseen events – to let go of a goal and take a new direction. Of course, this needs to be considered very, very carefully. Taking the decision to abandon a goal spontaneously or due to emotional disappointment should be ruled out completely.

In this connection, Senge describes a dangerous dynam-ic that always develops when important and large-scale goals are pursued that cannot be realized immediately. Initially a gap develops between the goal and the pres-ent reality, which is perceived as creative tension.

"The gap between vision and current reality is also a source of energy... We call this gap creative tension."
Peter M. Senge

The activities engaged in to reduce this tension, to achieve the goal, cannot, of course, always lead to immediate success. On the contrary, we often find our-selves facing delays, goals recede into the distance, and frustration and stress develop. What was initially (positively experienced) creative tension thus becomes (unpleasant) emotional tension (fear of failure, drop in self-esteem). A commonly perceived possibility of reducing the pressure that has developed consists in adapting the goal to "the realities," or diminishing it. In such cases we initially feel relief. But the price for this reduction of pressure is high: a small goal loses its fascination, the motivation it has generated is lessened, and we have less energy at our disposal. A negative spiral thus develops. Due to the reduction of impetus we experience further delays, the strength to overcome obstacles is lessened, and the goal is diminished again with the same consequences as before. Ultimately this

"Ultimately every person reaches every goal. He just has to lower his sights enough."
Hans Söhnker

further increases the level of stress, because even a lesser goal has not been achieved. All this is often played out very subtly in many small steps rather than in terms of the rather crude model presented here.

"The dynamics of
compromise lead
to mediocrity."
Peter M. Senge

"Gradually we give up our dreams and renounce the relationships we would like, the work that satisfies us and the better world we would like to live in." (Senge) "This is the dynamic of compromise, the path to mediocrity."

We have to learn to put up with the emotional tension, to comprehend setbacks as incentives, obstacles not as problems but as challenges, as opportunities for a FLOW experience. Those who do not give up and do not allow their own claims to sap their confidence will ultimately gain enormous strength. *"Endurance is the common denominator of all successful people."* Patience and perseverance are the foundation of self-motivation.

Endurance is a
talisman for life.
African saying

Senge also points to a further dynamic that can fatally prevent us from reaching our goals.

At first, a goal inspires and motivates; we move in the direction of our goal optimistically and get our first positive results. However, the closer we come to achieving a goal, the more another force pulls us back to the old reality, and thus, it becomes increasingly difficult to reach the goal the closer to our grasp it comes. The "rubber band" of creative tension that draws us in the direction of the goal loses elasticity the closer we come to our goal. On the other hand, the "security band" that pulls us back in the direction of our point of departure becomes stronger the shorter the distance to the goal. Therefore, it is very common for something to occur just before reaching the goal that throws us back, or even causes us to completely abandon the goal.

If the human being
had persistence,
nothing would be
impossible.
Chinese saying

Faced with structural conflicts like these, pure willpower is not enough to reach a solution. It is more likely to be the case that the problems will appear ever greater unless we deal with the causes of these internal obstacles. When we do, deeply entrenched internal blockages that, in some cases, we have been carrying around

(unconsciously) since our childhood or that have become fixed through force of habit, start to come to the
surface.

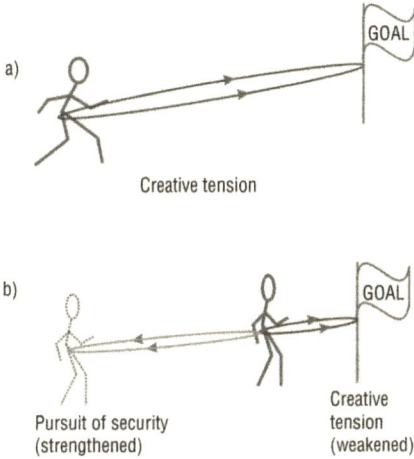

Figure 26: Creative tension versus the pursuit of security (based on Senge)

Often such blockages are based on fundamental views
of our own powerlessness or worthlessness. These are
probably an unavoidable concomitant of the process of
growing up. As children we inevitably have boundaries set for us and learn that not everything is possible and not all wishes can become reality. This necessary process of adaptation to reality, which involves saying goodbye to the "magical child," with its fantasies
of omnipotence in which everything is possible, leads
to a disproportionate generalization that ultimately
gives rise to the conviction that things which mean a
lot to us are unattainable.

Structures of human thought can be understood as complex, self-maintaining systems. Such systems, which
ensure our survival, are extraordinarily conservative
and continually create both internal and external circumstances that have proved suitable for survival in the
past. (However unpleasant prevailing circum-   stances
may be, the system is oriented to effectiveness rather
than quality.)

If we want to change these structures because they are proving too great an obstacle to the attainment of happiness, we have to make it clear to our system that the state we aspire to is also safe and suitable for survival. This can result in a long process in which the old basic assumptions are gradually displaced by new, more attractive experiences and the generalizations resulting from them. Apart from patience and perseverance, this process needs to be driven forward by a good measure of awareness and courage.

If we constructively engage with the developing tension and, thereby, are able to resist the cycle that leads to adaptation to external pressure, we can learn to see obstacles as steps on the path to a fulfilled and self-motivated life.

It is possible to utilize these emotional tensions in order to:

- actually reach our goals

- gain more awareness of ourselves and our actions

- expand our worldview

- gain greater maturity

- and thereby deal better with our lives

In order to attain genuinely intrinsic self-motivation it is necessary to deal with our own feelings and their origins. The process by which we develop awareness leads via the perception (not the suppression or evaluation) of all emotional aspects.

A precondition is the preparedness to look at one's "more unpleasant sides," such as fears, feelings of inferiority, and anger, and to deal flexibly with changing conditions in our surroundings. In the first place, this means confronting our reality at a fundamental level.

Dealing with fundamental assumptions

Breaking the "conservative rubber band" (see Figure 26, p. 205)

Once we have established our personal and profession-al goals we often find that, now and again, there is an accumulation of "accidents," setbacks, and negative feelings that seem peculiar because they completely contradict the positive, general mood that has been generated by the goal-setting process. The simple sug-gestion made by many successful books, to respond to such negativity with "positive thinking" and simple affirmations, is usually of no help at all. On the contra-ry, when we try such an approach, we often find that the situation really becomes acute, with the result that we start to doubt everything. In this chapter you will become acquainted with the Core Belief Process (devel-oped by Marc Allen and Shakti Gawain). This ap-proach can help to free you from restrictive viewpoints and obstructive mental models. This process is neces-sary before positive thinking can have any effect at all.

Simple positive thinking can produce the opposite.

"Core beliefs" are made up of fundamental assumptions, convictions, facts of experience, etc.

When we set ourselves a goal that inspires us, we chal-lenge ourselves to change our current situation, to grow and to enter a new terrain. As soon as we leave our safe harbor to sail the oceans, forms of emotional resistance that we have never experienced before sur-face and urge us to return to the place we have come from (old job, living situation, partner). As uncomfort-able as we may have felt in our previous situation, it has the advantage of being familiar. Everything that now lies before us is strange and gives rise to stress and irrational feelings. Sometimes we are aware of this, but often it is played out deep within our mind-set, and, indeed, there is a range of good reasons for continuing or repeating old, outgrown convictions.

"Growth is a process of creative destruction." Joseph Alois Schumpeter

A great goal can give rise to correspondingly great re-sistance, and this can lead to failure despite the fact that, at a conscious level, we have felt very happy that the goal was about to be reached.

Something that can help here is self-discipline. Every time the things you are familiar with beckon invitingly, you should automatically think of the most depressing situation associated with the job, living situation, or partner (or whatever else should be changed). However, this in itself is not enough.

It is important that we identify the background that informs these setbacks in order to gain a clear picture of the unpleasant emotions that are peculiarly linked with our momentum towards a better future – to accept them and engage with them directly so that we are able to identify the way they work. Such emotions might include fear of failure, fear of change, fear of not being liked, of being alone, of embarrassing situations, etc.

Adults often live within the limits of their childhood.

Changing your inner "should"-dimensions.

Where do these fears come from? We come to know our world as tiny, helpless beings. There is much that is threatening, and many of our experiences cause pain and sadness. We remember this and develop survival strategies to deal with these situations. These strategies are based on, among other things, *fundamental assumptions and core beliefs* regarding what the world is like, what other people are like, but also, what we ourselves are like. A certain "knowledge" is stored within us concerning how much love we are worthy of, what we are permitted to experience, how good, intelligent, hard-working, worthy of reward, deserving, cabable of reaching a certain goal we are – or not. Whether we want it to or not, our unconscious steers the process of living such that our experiences are framed by these fundamental assumptions. The highly complex system of the human being is programmed with control data that demands compliance, irrespective of how this makes us feel. As far as the unconscious is concerned, the only thing that matters is that we have survived till now.

When these fundamental assumptions or SHOULD parameters are "threatened" by the realization of a certain Goal Scenario, the basic need for our system to maintain stability ensures that the SHOULD parameters are maintained and reconfirmed, and not that the goal is realized.

Anyone wanting to actually realize their goals should use the following process to first identify fundamental assumptions that restrict their scope for action. This, in turn, allows us to consciously separate ourselves from these assumptions, and ultimately, enables our new SHOULD parameters to take effect. It is important to track down potentially disruptive factors and to deprive them of their efficacy.

However, the first step consists in completely accepting yourself as you are now, and not regarding these negative elements and feelings as something bad that must be eradicated. These feelings are completely legitimate. They warn you that something is not right. They create the need to find remedies; they push you to keep going until the things are clear. What we need to rid ourselves of is the repeated activation of the pattern that gives rise to these feelings.

I am
completely fine.

It is not important to get to the actual origins of everything. What you need to do is find out what sort of hidden notions are floating around in your head. These sorts of fundamental dogmas give rise to the mental processes, which, in turn, shape reality. We create a considerable portion of our own experience by repeating long-establishing patterns of thinking and behaving as a way of maintaining stability.

The Core Belief Process (based on the work of Marc Allen and Shakti Gawain)

Rituals can help
the self-motivation
process.

In order to develop a particular ritual of leave-taking and new beginnings from this process, this exercise includes precise instructions concerning the division and use of a sheet of paper (A4), which you should now have ready. You will also need whatever you usually write with and other paper for writing on, or a book you can use for this kind of work.

Rituals

Rituals are symbolic actions in which particular things are consciously reinforced and recognized in terms of their place in reality. Rituals can be momentous (e.g., weddings) or small, daily habits (e.g., a cup of tea or coffee in the morning). They have been used throughout human history. To achieve a high level of self-motivation, it is useful to create several rituals for yourself that you regularly practice. It is decisive for the effect of the ritual that you are clear about its content and meaning (e.g., a cup of tea in the morning – generates a sense of calm and allows you to collect your thoughts.)

Take some time somewhere you will not be disturbed. Put aside your sheet of A4 paper – you will only need it for Steps 7 and 8. Make sure your breathing is regular and calm and consciously relax yourself on every outward breath. Think about the particular problem you would like to solve, the area of life that you would like to improve, or in which you continue to find yourself confronting obstacles.

(Examples: The month always has too many days for the amount of money available. Or: there is never enough time. Or the man who appeared on the chat show who has broken 29 bones over the years and each year has had to spend four to six weeks in hospital. His system works on the basic assumption that the world is dangerous; he breaks bones but this is how he survives. A fatal SHOULD dimension. Or the dialog you have with yourself based on: "Nobody

likes me." Anyone who works on this basic assumption will always act as a magnet for people who do not really value him or her. Or: I'm not a sporty type, I always eat too much, I can't learn foreign languages, etc., etc. That's enough examples. In which area of your life would you like to rid yourself of an unnecessary, self-restricting basic assumption?

Step 1: Describing the problem

Describe the nature of the problem, the situation or the area of life, which you would like to solve or change for the better. Take three to five minutes to write out everything that generally occurs to you.

Step 2: What are your feelings in this context?

Name the specific feelings you have in this context such as fear, sadness, anger, guilt, shame, etc. However, do not include thoughts about these feelings or the problem.

Step 3: What physical sensations do you experience?

Step 4: What thoughts do you have in this context?

What negative thoughts automatically pass through your mind? What sort of apprehensions, fears and worries come up? Take a few minutes to write down your thoughts.

Step 5: Inducing the preparedness to change the brain by imagining negative scenarios.

a) What is the worst that could happen in this area? What is your worst fear?

b) If the worst happens, what are you most afraid of? What is the worst-case scenario?

c) What would it be like if this actually happened? What would be the worst consequence? What would be the worst, worst case (for you and the people who are close to you, or who have a particular significance for you?) Let out a deep breath and let go of all these negative feelings.

Step 6: What is the best thing that could happen?

Describe your ideal solution, the "optimal scenario" in this area of your life.

Step 7: What is behind all this?

a) What fears or negative basic assumptions are preventing you from achieving what you actually want to in this area of your life (Step 6)?

Once you have discovered this pattern, briefly and vividly describe in writing this negative basic assumption about yourself or the world. If you discover several negative assumptions, list them one under another on a sheet of paper. You should go through all the following steps in relation to each of the basic assumptions, up to and including Step 9. First, identify what you see as the most influential negative basic assumption and proceed with b).

b) Now take the A4 sheet of paper, fold it across the middle and then above and below, 2 cm from the edge (see illustration).

Negative Basic Assumption

Smooth out the sheet of paper as shown below and write out the negative sentence in the 2-cm field at the top.

c) Now turn the sheet of paper 90 degrees to the horizontal. In the empty left-hand field, use keywords to describe situations that confirm this negative basic assumption in reality.

Negative Basic Assumption	Negative Examples		

d) Take a short pause and ask yourself: what was all that? Was it all so bad? Or was there at some point a tiny exception? Look for those moments in your life in relation to the area concerned when things turned out as you would want them to. Describe these moments using keywords in the right-hand field. Do not use the outer right-hand (2 cm) field. Only once you are sure that you cannot remember anything else, focus your imagination on generating situations in which everything turns out as you would want it to.

Negative Basic Assumption	Negative Examples	Positive Examples	

Take the time to re-read the keywords describing positive situations, and then think of a sentence or statement, which contains a positive basic assumption that could evoke such a situation.

Step 8: Your personal affirmation

Now turn the sheet of paper to the vertical so that the remaining empty 2-cm field is at the top. Write your positive affirmation in this field.

Positive Basic Assumption
Positive Examples
Negative Examples
Negative Basic Assumption

Affirmation

An affirmation is a powerful, reinforcing confirmation in the form of a statement. It corrects a negative belief and nullifies it. The statement must be positively phrased and may not contain negations. (Words like "not," "no," "without," and "free of," and words starting with the prefix "un" should not be used!) The affirmation should be brief, as simple as possible, and meaningful for you.

Examples:

"I am a worthwhile person. I have earned my success."

Affirmations are a simple method of strengthening new doctrines.

Use the present tense, as if what you want is happening right now:

"I am experiencing fullness and richness in my life."
The affirmation should express the opposite of your negative basic assumption. Transform your negative thoughts into something powerful and positive.

Negative basic assumption: "I just don't have enough time to do the things I want to."

Affirmation: "I have more than enough time to do all the things that are up to me."

Negative statement: "The world is dangerous."

Affirmation: "I am living in a safe, wondrous world."

Negative basic assumption: "I always have to struggle to survive."

Affirmation: "I am totally successful in realizing my intentions in a way that is easy and positive for all those involved." (This is suitable for more advanced affirmations. Don't be afraid of starting with a simple formulation, which you can refine later.)

The affirmation should sound coherent for you personally when you read it aloud and evoke a powerful, positive feeling. If this isn't the case, take the time to change it until it has this effect for you.)

Now tear off the left half of the sheet of paper with the negative examples and negative basic assumptions and destroy it. (Burning this piece of paper has proved particularly effective. But take care you only burn the paper!)

We are not trying to work magic here, and the process doesn't stop with Step 8. The real work comes now, with Step 9.

Step 9: Repetition as a key to success

The effect of
your affirmation
is increased by
regular use.

*Read out your personal affirmations several times a day
and write them out repeatedly.*

*While you do this, use your imagination to picture in
detail the development of your ideal situation.*

*If you think it can work for you, adopt the discipline of
writing out your affirmation ten times every day, until
you have the impression that it has become part of your
own positive belief structure. Use the reverse side of the
piece of paper to record negative thoughts, inner defensive-
ness, and emotional resistances. Continue writing out
the affirmations until you no longer feel any emotional
resistance to this exercise. Continue destroying the sheets
of paper until you no longer experience negative
thoughts, in other words, until the reverse side is empty.
At this point, you can conclude the exercise.*

*This ritual is one of the most powerful instruments in the
processes of change we have discussed.*

Date for my first Core Belief Process:

_____

Energy 4: Resisting the appeal of urgency

"Only a conscious decision for what is important prevents an unconscious decision for what is unimportant."
                                        Stephen R. Covey

Even if we are conscious of our values and have set clear goals, it can still be the case that an overload in private or professional life can produce motivation gaps. We no longer feel equal to the flood of activities surging around us and find ourselves working frantically and without motivation. Yet, as Stephen Covey warns: *"Doing more things faster is no substitute for doing the right things."*

"Doing more things faster is no substitute for doing the right things." *Stephen Covey*

There are two methods that can help you experience your day in a way that is self-motivated and subject to your focused and purpose oriented ATTENTION:

• A clear distinction between urgent and important things – the Eisenhower method

• Complete concentration on the present moment – Ivy Lee's six-point plan for the day

You can drastically improve the ratio between effort and result if you are able to develop a clear sense of the difference between what is important and what is urgent, and then establish a relationship between the two categories that makes sense.

The optimization of personal effectiveness can also be facilitated by focusing attention on the individual day, and, above all, on the task that you are facing at a given time. The two following approaches have withstood the test of time. They are simple to use and are among the most valuable tools that we can offer. While the major part of this book represents a bigger one-off project, several aspects of which can be refreshed once a year, the last two chapters are devoted to daily tasks, to the uses that this book can offer you that apply to every day of your life.

Make a clear distinction between what is urgent and what is important

Many people approach these two concepts fairly indiscriminately.

Something that is urgent puts us under pressure. It wants to be dealt with quickly.

Urgency is connected with *pressure*. Something that is urgent puts pressure on us. It generates tension, an internal state of pressure, and causes alarm for our protective system. The state of excitation of our limbic system, an area of the brain beneath the cerebrum, is increased, and alarm and activity hormones are secreted. The limbic system is responsible for our feelings of pleasure and displeasure. And in the case of urgency, we are dealing with feelings of displeasure. We experience a strong inner urge to be rid of the undesirable state of tension as quickly as possible.

Everything that appears urgent to us has an inherent tendency to be dealt with.

Most information impulses connected with urgency produce massive excitation in our nervous system. Such impulses are visible, audible, and tangible. (The ringing of a telephone, the raised or shouting voice of a superior, or an angry customer are acoustic signals, while a large stack of files on a desk, a meeting marked on a calendar, a fax that spills from the fax machine are tangible, optical stimuli that demand an immediate reduction of the tension associated with them.) As a result, urgent things have an inherent tendency to be dealt with quickly. Furthermore, when we deal with urgent things we appear to others to be efficient and we make ourselves popular. However, urgent things are not always important and very often, they are even unimportant!

"Because we are always reachable, we are often present and absent at the same time."
Lothar J. Seiwert

The simplest example of this is the ringing of a telephone. The sound of a phone causes many people, regardless of the importance of what they are doing, to rush to the receiver, pick it up, and in so doing, stop the ringing. In private life, the question "Who is calling me?" can also play a role. However, in working life, in the professional world, our actual concern is usually only to be rid of the unpleasant sensation caused by the ringing, even if, at the time, we might be in the middle of an important face-to-face discussion.

This is a typical example of the how something urgent can overlay something important. A stack of papers not yet dealt with that are lying on a desk and causing disorder can also generate a feeling of urgency within us, with the result that we might say to ourselves: "First I'll get rid of these and then I'll start the project." The result can be that we spend three months, three years, or 30 years working through stacks of papers and, in the worst case, never actually get around to what is really important.

Longstanding experience reveals that many people spend the majority of their day dealing with urgent things and only get to the important part of their work in the evening or even have to take work home with them on the weekends. Such people often feel drained and find that they enjoy their work less and less.

But what is important? *Important* – the word is originally transferred from the Latin word "importare" . That means "bring in". Important things are things with something additional within them; things that have meaning, things that have value and make sense. Nothing is important in itself. We, or others, "bring in" or give a special meaning, a purpose to a certain thing (e.g. an intention, a conversation, or an appointment) according to a certain value structure and the goals that follow from it. Importance rests on conscious and/or unconscious decision-making processes, for instance, on activities of the cerebrum, and within these processes feeling can also play a role in how things are valued. However, such decisions do not necessarily give rise to impulses promoting action.

> Tasks take on importance through values and goals.

> Important things often tend to be put aside.

Important things, therefore, do not have an inherent tendency to be dealt with quickly. Important things tend rather to be put aside because there are always a few urgent matters to which our unconscious system gives priority.

Important matters that are not also urgent do not put pressure on us. They do not create a mood of alarm, and often they do not even mobilize our ATTENTION in a particular way. Dealing with something important requires personal initiative, spontaneous effort, overcoming habit, or lethargy.

When we do not have an exact idea of what is important, when our goals are unclear or contradictory, then distractions become stronger and we tend to devote our time to dealing with what seems urgent.

Important things are above all those things that serve the realization and/or maintenance of a value.

Examples:
1. Personal, private value system
2. Personal, professional value system
   Value system of people close to us (family, friends, etc.)
4. Value system of the company/enterprise
5. Value system of third parties

It follows that important things are also those which serve the achievement of a goal, since the achievement of goals means the realization of values. Values and the goals derived from them are ordered hierarchically:

Examples of types of goals:

1. Enterprise goal
2. Sector/departmental goal
3. Goal of superior / project leader
4. Goal of one or more colleagues
5. Own professional goal
6. Own private (compatible with professional) goal
7. Own private (at odds with professional) goal
8. Private goals of others

If we are not clear about our value system and if we do not go through the process of setting goals, it is not possible to make decisions on priorities regarding what is important.

The trick is to shade what is important with the "color of urgency." This is the reason that we recommend you attach a date to your goal scenario. This creates urgency. "Reading aloud" the goal scenario to yourself twice a day also creates corresponding feelings of displeasure as long as your prevailing reality and the desired reality of the goal scenario you have read out deviate from one another.

The trick is to shade what is important with the "color of urgency."

(It is worth noting here that the secret of the art of leadership consists in leaders making what they consider important appear as urgent in the minds of those working with them.

And if you want to lead yourself, to motivate yourself, then this is achieved most effectively when you make what you consider important also urgent and when you do not wait for external circumstances or third parties to do this for you. Here too, our ATTENTION, *our consciousness, is called upon.)*

You have possibly noticed that a much-loved and commonly used word has not yet appeared. What about things that are "interesting"?

Surely it is when we are dealing with things that awaken our interest that we show true mastery. It can be precisely those things that move us, that provide us with clear indications of our value system, which can, in turn, become important. On the other hand, it is precisely interesting things that can conceal the traps that others lay for us in order to divert our ATTENTION to the pursuit of their interests, thus robbing us of our time (if not of our money.)

We have come, full circle back to the point at which we began this book in order to live a life of purpose: everything that is interesting requires our very careful ATTENTION. Only a mind that is aware of the difference between important and unimportant, between urgent and non-urgent, can separate the wheat from the chaff in a matter of seconds, and can pursue what is both interesting *and* important **while saying NO to what is merely interesting but not really important**. *And we need to be aware that often people make something important for them into something urgent for those around them*

We have come full circle and return to the theme of ATTENTIVENESS.

by alarming their sensory nervous and limbic systems. We therefore need to be clear about what can justifiably be regarded as urgent.

Examples of different types of urgency:

1. Something has to be undertaken immediately in order to save life.
2. Something has to be undertaken immediately because the existence of the enterprise/company is under threat.
3. Something has to be undertaken because one's own professional existence is threatened.
4. Immediate action is required because a large contract/task is threatened.
5. Immediate action is required because a customer relationship is under threat.
6. Immediate action is necessary to keep open or safeguard future options for the enterprise/company.
7. Immediate action is necessary to keep open or safeguard one's own professional future.
8. Immediate action is necessary to improve opportunities.
9. An immediate reaction is necessary to avoid impeding in-house communication / the relationship with higher parts of the hierarchy.
10. Immediate action is required to restore or maintain one's own well-being.

Whenever *something interesting* comes up, put a check on your immediate reactions and examine whether what is interesting is also important. It is only after doing this that you should either take action or decide that, although interesting, the matter is unimportant and you can forget about it.

You need to create an internal monitor to avoid ending in a "treadmill" situation.

How do we approach the everyday world with this knowledge?

In the first place, you should try to develop an everyday sensitivity for what is important or unimportant and urgent or not urgent.

Over three or four days, take the time to classify one entire day's activities using the "life coordinates cross" below – which represents a modified version of the method developed by General and later President Eisenhower to differentiate priorities within the hectic framework of everyday life.

If something is important and urgent – such as crisis management, large-scale projects with imminent dead-lines, pressing everyday problems, a tax declaration that must be submitted – it belongs, for example, in the top-left **quadrant (I)**.

Things that are urgent but not important – a series of conferences and meetings in which participation is urgent but only really important for some of the parti-cipants, certain urgent phone calls, part of the mail that has been delivered, unimportant but urgent matters in which you invest time without resulting in an effect, things that have no connection to the realization of your own, or another, goal – then it belongs in the lower-left **quadrant (II)**.

Lost living time: Quadrant III.

Things that are neither important nor urgent – which include everything trivial such as reading the paper, indiscriminately watching television, some items of mail that you read and immediately throw away, cer-tain phone calls you make because someone has left a message on the answering machine without really requiring a return call, and a whole range of other forms of time-wasting, which are ultimately pleasant activities without further consequences – belong in the lower-right **quadrant (III)**.

Things that are important but not absolutely urgent – all activities that you undertake to promote your own potential, such as developing a goal scenario, drawing up a plan, maintaining or extending your own pro-ductive capacity or that of the enterprise, discovering new possibilities, and everything else that has to do with establishing, maintaining, and deepening rela-tionships to other people and other organizations, and the important area of regeneration, recuperation, and energy generation, activities that are important but, as a rule, not urgent – should be placed in the upper-right **quadrant (IV)**.

You can make a copy of this life coordinates cross and, for example, put it on your desk or hang it on your wall so that you can refer to it throughout the day and ask yourself:

- What am I doing at the moment? In which quadrant am I located at present?

- And in which quadrant am I predominantly active?

I
IV

important

urgent   not
                                                                   urgent

II
III

unimportant

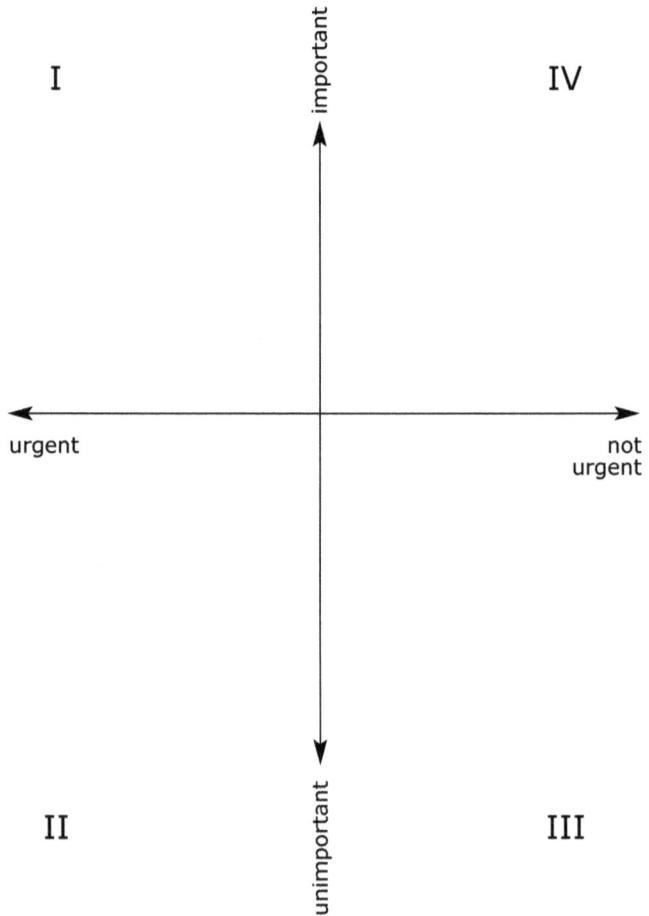

Figure 27: Life coordinates cross

However, there is also a much more precise way to use this tool:

Every time you change to another activity, draw a dot in the appropriate quadrant and try to estimate approximately what position of the dot most accurately reflects the character of the activity. By doing this you will gradually produce a profile of the individual day or several days, and you will be able to recognize where the emphases of your activities lie.

You have here an easy-to-use personal feedback system, which provides you with the truth about what you are doing with your life. Be prepared for surprises ...

Watch out!
Danger!

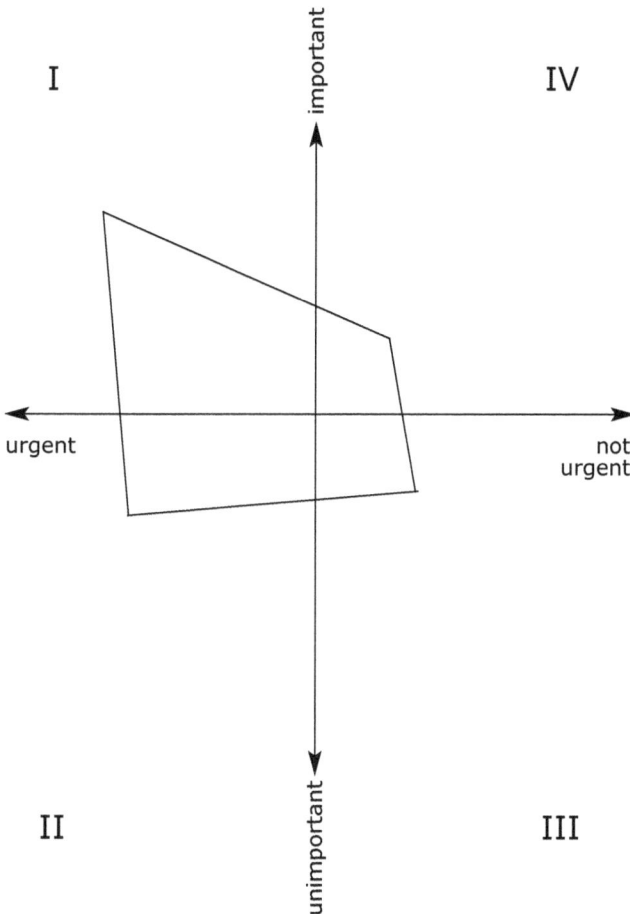

Figure 28: Profile of the troubleshooter

One danger is that you are engaging too often and for too long in Quadrant I *(figure 28, page 227)*. People who constantly have to prove themselves by managing crises and who devote too much time in a day to dealing with situations in Quadrant I can no longer plan, neglect their interpersonal relationships, and can no longer regenerate themselves. Possible consequences are permanent stress, total exhaustion, burn-out syndrome, depressions, and other serious illnesses.

The reaction that immediately suggests itself, namely

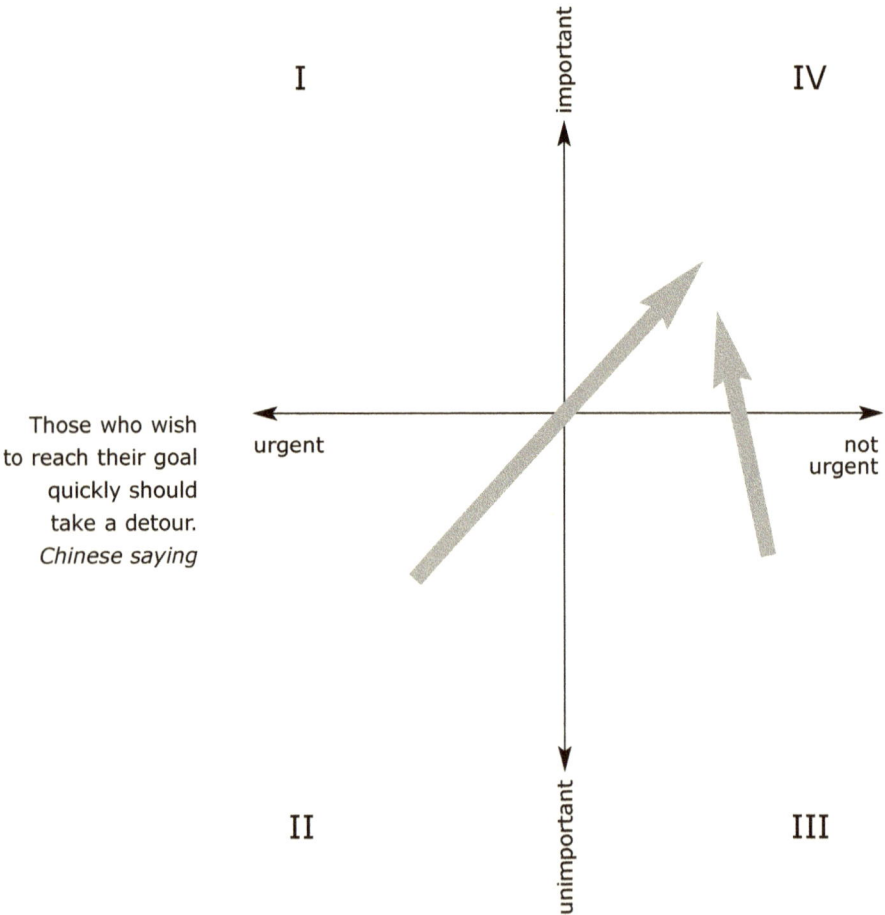

The reaction that immediately suggests itself – protect yourself from over-strict time management!

Those who wish to reach their goal quickly should take a detour. *Chinese saying*

I

IV

important

urgent   not urgent

unimportant

II

III

Figure 29: Time reserves can only be mobilized in the two lower Quadrants II and III can.

to do less in Quadrant I and more in Quadrant IV, is hardly possible in practice. Once we find ourselves tied into Quadrant I, we can't simply leave something out. As soon as we start to reduce our activities here, we find ourselves facing massive problems, which ultimately force us to engage even more intensively in crisis management. Quadrant I contains all the activities that are both important and urgent. If we leave something out then something that is both important and urgent will not get done, and this causes problems, which, ultimately, also have to be solved.

There are people who simply say: I can't do this anymore. I've got to get out of this dangerous situation. I'm simply going to do less. I'm going to stop work at 5:30 p.m. and devote myself to my family. Two weeks later these same people find that they have no time at all for their family. They are faced with so many burning problems that they can only run around with a fire extinguisher in their hand.

What does the solution look like? The solution – and it is the only one – lies in reducing the **activities** in **Quadrant II** (and of course also those in **Quadrant III.**)

This means doing fewer things that are urgent but not important. This is easier said than done. When we are not engaged in activities that do not have a high degree of importance or are clearly unimportant – activities that locate us just above or below the horizontal axis of the coordinates cross – then we find ourselves in an overlapping field where the non-important and important can come into very close proximity.

If we want to reduce the profile in Quadrants II and III, we can only achieve this by **precisely selecting between what is important and what is unimportant.** *(see figure 29, page 228).* The **clarity of the distinction** is shown by the simple picture: everything in the coordinates cross that lies above the horizontal line is important. Everything below this line is unimportant. Important activities are thus those in Quadrant IV and all those that serve the realization of goals (Quadrant I).

Train your concentration daily – take some time for your fourth quadrant.

We can, therefore, only make a strict distinction between what is important and what is unimportant when we have clear ideas of our goals, which make it possible to differentiate between Quadrants I and II. When someone has goals or a goal, he knows that everything which moves him in the direction of realizing this goal is important. Everything that does not lead in this direction is not important (with the exception of the activities in Quadrant IV). These are clear criteria that enable us to distinguish what is important from what is unimportant.

Quality of life is generated in Quadrant IV. Do more things that are important but not urgent.

People with no clear idea of their goals slide almost inevitably into Quadrant II. Most of their time is devoted to things that either do not lead towards a goal or do not belong in Quadrant IV. Commonly such activities involve pressing matters, and due to the confusion between urgent and important, these people are convinced that they are dealing with important things on the grounds that they are engaged in hectic activity.

By contrast, people who have a clear idea of their goals can significantly reduce the amount of time they spend in Quadrant II and increase the time they devote to Quadrant IV.

Soon you will find you are experiencing the pressure of urgent things less and less.

The more time we spend in this sphere, the more time we have for the prevention of crises, the targeted improvement of our own effectiveness, the cultivation of our relationships, the development of new ideas, and our own regeneration and recuperation. In order to experience what this rather indirect approach can produce in terms of directly beneficial consequences, you should take the time as soon as possible to "locate" yourself in Quadrant IV and to consider: *What do I actually want? What is important for me? What are the values in my life that I would like to realize?*

"Quality of life," writes Covey, who worked with the Eisenhower system and developed it further, "grows out of the moments in which we manage not to react automatically to a stimulus that reaches our system but instead insert a small pause for thought in which we consider in a split second whether what we are about to do is important, urgent, or both."

If it is only urgent but not important we should not do it. Here, we need to say categorically "no" within ourselves (and where necessary to the outside world) and instead, do something that takes us forward.

Energy 5: Mastering the day by purposeful action

"Compared with the ability to meaningfully order the work of a single day, everything else in life is child's play."
Johann Wolfgang von Goethe

Every day is a new unit of your life. Through the shaping of each day you decide – whether consciously or unconsciously – how your life will be. If you wish to experience your life as something valuable you must experience every day as meaningful, in other words, you must realize your values and principles and not allow yourself to be steered by others in one direction today, and then another tomorrow. As you saw in the last chapter, you first have to make yourself aware and be able, at any one time, to distinguish important actions from unimportant ones. But how do we manage to do this amidst the hectic pace of daily life? This requires skilful mixture of craft and art, the kind of combination that historically made a master craftsman a master. We see that even Goethe had to make an effort in this regard, and at that time, there were neither e-mails nor controllers nor direct transmissions of the current stock market rates! In other words, the pyramidal pressure was perhaps somewhat less, even if it is said that Goethe's boss had to strive constantly to keep him working.

Experience every day as a significant unit of life.

Clearly, this problem of mastering the individual day is not a new one. Yet there is a very simple solution, one that was already developed by management consultant Ivy Lee at the beginning of the 20th century when he presented it as a method of improving productivity to Charles Schwab, the president of Bethlehem Steel. Schwab found the idea so good that several months later, he sent Lee – with whom he had not agreed on a consultation fee – a check for 25,000 dollars *(which at the time corresponded to the value of a family home.)*

Here is the whole story. Mr. Lee had heard that the steel company was having certain problems and wanted to offer his services. He asked the president about the causes of the problems, but Schwab had no answer. The only thing he knew, said Schwab, was that the firm's output was becoming increasingly mediocre and turnover was decreasing. He was certain that this had nothing to do with his knowledge and abilities. What he was looking for were possible ways of also intensifying his output.

Mr. Lee answered that he could explain to Mr. Schwab in 20 minutes how he could increase his success by at least 50%. He then handed the astounded president an empty sheet of paper and said:

"Write down on this piece of paper the six most important things you are planning to do tomorrow."

The president did this in around three minutes. Then Mr. Lee asked him to number the six points *in order of importance*. This took another five minutes. Then Mr. Lee told the president to put the piece of paper in his pocket. Finally he said:

"First thing tomorrow morning take the paper out of your pocket and look at task one. Don't worry about the others, just the first one. Then start to work on it and stay with it until it's complete.

Then go on to number two and do the same thing, then number three and so on until you reach the end of the day. Don't worry if you haven't been able to complete everything. You will have worked on the most important points – the others can wait. If you are not able to deal with them in this way, you won't be able to at all. Without a system you would not only require ten times as much time, you wouldn't have dealt with them in their order of importance."

"Do this every day," Lee continued, *"and if you are convinced of the value of the system, have your employees try it. Try out this method for a while and then send me a check. Pay me whatever you think the method is worth."*

This whole conversation did not last longer than a half hour. A few months later the president sent Mr. Lee a check for 25,000 dollars. In the letter accompanying the check Schwab wrote, *"Your idea was the most profitable I have encountered in my whole career."*

However, this method was not only simple. Above all, it proved enduringly practicable. The president and his employees worked according to the method and within five years the firm prospered. What was, at the time, a small, unknown steel company became the largest independent steel producer in the world.

In this way you can gain time for the really important things in your life:

Step 1: Plan your tasks in detail without exception the evening before.

As soon as you have decided at the end of your working day that you are now stopping work and having some leisure time, take ten minutes to write down on a blank sheet of paper (or perhaps in your appointments diary) everything you still have to do, or what you want to do, the following day. You are thus making a list of things not yet dealt with that are important to you.

Step 1:
At the end of the working day plan the next one.

Step 2: Find the six most important things

Then decide what the six most important things are that you would like to, must, or can deal with the following day. Use the melon principle here: divide the individual intentions and projects into small steps and decide on a well-defined task unit for the next day. After all, we would never simply bite into a large uncut watermelon. That would hurt our teeth and the green skin and the white layer under it would not provide us with any refreshment. Therefore, don't write: *"Remodel attic,"* but rather: *"Make appointment with architect."*

Step 2:
Select the six most important points.

Step 3: Establish an order

**Step 3:
Rank the six
points in order of
importance.**

Then consider the order in which you want to, or must, deal with these six points. This is the step that most people forget to take. They simply write down their points one under the other as they occur to them. Establishing priorities the evening before makes a decisive difference.

You thus need to ask yourself: What is the most important, what is the second most important? And continue until you reach the end. When you have established the order, write it down on a second piece of paper or transfer the points to your diary or computer.

Step 4: Concentrate only on one activity

**Step 4:
Work through the
points in order.
Only work on one
point at a time
and concentrate
on each one until
it has been dealt
with.**

The following day, as soon as you have some time outside of your standard schedule, start with the first task on your six-point list. Do not pay any attention to points two to six. Concentrate exclusively on completing the first task. Work on this as long as it takes to complete it or until the next interruption comes, for example, a pre-arranged meeting, which you have to attend. The only other reason for interrupting your work is if you find you are missing something you need to complete the task at hand (e.g. if you need information which you are not able to get at the moment or you have to wait for the completion of a certain element by others.) Otherwise the principle applies: you keep working on the first task until it is complete! You do not need to worry that you might not complete the second, third, or fourth task, since with this method you can always be sure you are at least getting the most important task under control.

It takes a certain amount of experience – you should reckon with three to six weeks – to get to the point where, in the case of bigger projects, you will find that you can define the task elements making up your six points in a way that does not result in other important things being left unattended to. The real art lies in the skilful division of tomorrow's tasks shortly before ending your day.

Step 5: Proceeding step by step

Once you have completed the first task, examine your priorities once again and begin with number two on your list. In most cases, particularly when one is just beginning to use this method, one only manages to complete two or three things on the list. In the evening you will sit down with the general list again and find there are points that need to be added and others that can be taken away. Then make up another six-point list for the following day. And so the process continues. You will see that after a few days, some things that were initially in the fifth or sixth position will have moved to the first or second position and will thus ultimately be dealt with. But you will also be surprised to find that there are points that remain in the fourth or fifth position for five or six days before being crossed off the list altogether, because you have realized in the meantime that they are not really that important or that they have solved themselves due to one circumstance or another. You will realize that it would have been a pity to invest even five minutes of your energy in these task areas.

This method has proved itself over the decades and, apart from its enormous efficacy, it has a wonderful additional effect. By focusing your attention on dealing with one task at a time you will create optimal possibilities for a FLOW experience.

And after a certain time, you will realize that because you are always engaged in something particularly important you will be less bothered by other people with banalities. It seems that people are capable of very refined perception and, because of what you radiate non-verbally and the way you communicate, people will realize that it is not appropriate to approach you with something that is not really important. You will reduce your stress levels because you will no longer be pushing a mountain of things you have not dealt with around in front of you. We cannot do everything; the limits on our time limit our possibilities. However, if you do everything that is important,

Step 5:
Continually check priorities, but don't let yourself be distracted. Only work on one task at a time.

approach your goals step by step, and experience achievement as part of a process, you will gain a deep feeling of satisfaction. If, one day, you can say, "By and large I have managed to take the way of the heart," then we can shake hands across the barriers of space and time and say: It was worth it! – for us, the work of writing, and for you, the endurance you have shown in reading and working on your self-motivation. For one thing is certain, as Catherine of Siena (1347–1380) knew:

"It is not beginning that is rewarded but solely endurance."

However, without a beginning there can be no later reward. We wish you the enterprising spirit that will continually lead you into new things, for in the words of Hermann Hesse *"... in every beginning dwells some magic that protects us and helps us to live."*

PART III

Appendices 1–4,
Acknowlededgment, Authors

Appendix 1:
Six special value lists for the following areas of life:

1. Personal growth
   (personal development), from page 243
2. Profession, career, company, from page 246
3. Personal relations, friendship, love, partner-ship, family, home, from page 249
4. Body, health, sport, fun, activities, holiday, recreation, from page 252
5. Financial aspects, possessions, assets, from page 255
6. Esteem through others, prestige, recognition, social role, from page 257

Checklist for your work with specific value lists B 1 – 6

Step 1:
Overview of the current values list

Step 2:
Expanding the values list with your own specific values

Step 3:
Selection of your six most important values

Step 4:
Ranking your values

Step 5:
Intermediate consideration – defining the differ-ence between intermediate and ultimate values

Step 6:
Identifying the degree of realization and visuali-zation – entering the six selected values in the center of the Integrity Wheel, expanding sectors, and filling the fields in accordance with the degree of satisfaction.

Once you have gone through these specific lists of values B1–B6 you can write the respective, most important values in to the form sheet on page 98.

From page 103 onwards, the process continues with developing a goal scenario in order to realize the values.

Step 7:
(Concentrating on fundamentals) Selecting a value that you want to take on a much greater significance in the next 12 to 18 months of your life

Once you have worked through the process several times, repeat step 7 using a time frame of five years and 15 years

Step 8:
Describing the meaning content of the selected values – formulating wishes

Step 9:
Making wishes reality – designing the goal scenario (for details see Focus 4: The Goal Scenario, p. 103 ff.)

You can find the checklists again to Steps 8 and 9 at the end of values list B6 (pages 258–270 and onwards).

B 1: Values list for personal growth (personality development)

O Self-confidence   O Composure

O Recognition   O Meaning

O Power   O Security

O Influence   O Freedom

O Honesty   O Attentiveness

O Acceptance by others   O Accepting others as they are

O Integrity   O Ability to deal with conflict

O Adventure   O Strength

O Creativity   O Success

O Personality   O Self-respect

O Flow   O Ability to be alone

O Living in the present   O Self-esteem

O Self-confidence   O Seeking/accepting challenges

O Trusting others   O Flexibility

O Knowledge   O Astuteness/wisdom

O Fun   O Responsibility

O Abundance   O Self-knowledge

O Enthusiasm   O Individuality

O Helping others   O Intuition

O Self-actualization   O Freedom of choice

O Order   O Freedom of action

O Realism   O Independence

O Justness   O Harmony

O Communication   O Friendship

O Contact with   O Ability to convince
  others   other people

O The feeling of   O Ability to take on
  being involved   risks

O Radiating   O Mastering foreign
  charisma   languages

O Having your life   O Courage of your own
  under control   convictions

O Knowing and   O Inner calm, inner
  experiencing your   peace
  own mission

O Solidarity   O (Self-) Discipline

O Belief   O Flexibility

O Punctuality   O Humour

O Idealism   O Altruism

O Competence   O Critical ability

O Religion   O Spirituality

O _____   O _____

My current six most important values in the B 1 area: Personal growth (personality development):

o _____

o _____

o _____

o _____

o _____

o _____

These values are currently ranked:

1. _____

2. _____

3. _____

4. _____

5. _____

6. _____

Date _____

Continuation: Transfer values to an Integrity Wheel with six sectors (see steps 6–9 in section A, p. 89 ff.) and then continue with Focus 4: The Goal Scenario (p. 103 ff.).

It is recommended that you download these pages from the Internet or make copies of the empty form so that you can update your list periodically.

B 2: Values list for: Profession, career, business

O Recognition	O Good salary
O Power	O Security
O Fascination	O Freedom
O Promotion	O Advancement opportunities
O Interesting tasks	O Good working conditions
O Learning opportunities	O Partnership
O Adventure	O Teamwork
O Competition	O Success
O Ecological orientation	O Influential position
O Loyalty	O Flow
O Independence	O Fun
O Harmony	O Responsibility
O Helping others	O Independence
O Creativity	O Challenge
O Self-actualization	O Freedom of choice
O Being part of a renowned firm	

Continued over page

O Comfort   O Fairness

O Competence   O Order

O Freedom of action O Enthusiasm

O People contact   O Convincingness

O Risk   O Command of time

O Quality   O Expertise

O High tempo   O Precision

O Routine   O Community

O Variety   O Leadership role

O Time pressure   O Friendships

O Ability to make decisions

O Physical challenge

O Work in the art field

O Work in the cultural field

O The feeling of being involved

O Support for personal problems

O Status / social esteem

O Work with social significance

O No pressure, low-level demand

O _____

My current six most important values in the area
B 2: Profession, career, business are:

O _____

O _____

O _____

O _____

O _____

O _____

These values are currently ranked:

1. _____

2. _____

3. _____

4. _____

5. _____

6. _____

Date _____

*Continuation: Transfer values to an Integrity Wheel with
six sectors (see steps 6–9 in section A, p. 89 ff.) and then
continue with Focus 4: The Goal Scenario (p. 103 ff.).*

*It is recommended that you download these pages from the
Internet or make copies of the empty form so that you can
update your list periodically.*

B 3: Values list for personal relationships, friendship, love, partnership, family, home

O Affection

O Love

O Marriage

O Dependence

O Children

O Security

O Belongingness

O Fun

O Friends

O Amorous adventure

O Intimacy

O Sexuality

O Learning

O Passion

O Tantra

O Security

O Partnership

O Flirting

O Family

O Power

O Leisure

O Home

O Calm

O Honesty

O Sharing

O Success

O Closeness

O Personal integrity

O Material wealth

O Spirituality

O Reliability

O Feeling of belonging

O Supporting, helping

O Protection from loneliness

O Platonic relationship

O Freedom from obligation

O Open relationship   O Exclusive relationship

O Being needed   O Being touched
physically

O Confrontation   O Conversation

O Caring for others

O Bond with parents

O Relationship with child/children

O Important friendships

O Popularity with the opposite sex

O Popularity with the same sex

O Engaging in a common cause

O – an idea

O – a project

O Being accepted as one is

O Being admired, idolized

O _____

O _____

O _____

O _____

O _____

O _____

O _____

My current six most important values in the B 3 area: Values list for personal relationships, friendship, love, partnership, family, home are:

O _____

O _____

O _____

O _____

O _____

O _____

These values are currently ranked:

1. _____

2. _____

3. _____

4. _____

5. _____

6. _____

Date _____

Continuation: Transfer values to an Integrity Wheel with six sectors (see steps 6–9 in section A, p. 89 ff.) and then continue with Focus 4: The Goal Scenario (p. 103 ff.).

It is recommended that you download these pages from the Internet or make copies of the empty form so that you can update your list periodically.

B 4: Values list for physique, health, sport, leisure time, holidays, recuperation and games

O Health

O Pleasure

O Leisure time

O Leisure

O Calm

O Recuperation

O Appearance

O Physical fitness

O Muscles

O Endurance

O Mobility

O Relaxation

O Creating art

O Reading

O Enjoying art

O Listening to music

O Manual skills

O Car

O Writing

O Making music

O Social contacts

O Games

O Massage

O Travel

O Cinema

O Theatre

O Opera

O Musicals

O Readings

O Art show openings

O Going for walks

O Bodybuilding

O Mountain climbing

O Jogging

O Trekking

O Swimming

Continued over page

O Tennis   O Golf

O Riding   O Flying

O Fencing   O Fishing

O Sailing   O Diving

O Martial arts   O Dancing

O Sauna   O Qi Gong

O Tai Chi   O Aikido

O Badminton   O Handicrafts

O Needlework   O Gardening

O Painting   O Sculpture

O Silk painting   O Photography

O Cooking   O Filming

O Computer games   O Bowling

O Doing nothing   O Singing

O _____

O _____

O _____

O _____

My current six most important values in the B 4 area: Values list for physique, health, sport, games, leisure time, holidays, recuperation are:

O _____

O _____

O _____

O _____

O _____

O _____

These values are currently ranked:

1. _____

2. _____

3. _____

4. _____

5. _____

6. _____

Date _____

Continuation: Transfer values to an Integrity Wheel with six sectors (see steps 6–9 in section A, p. 89 ff.) and then continue with Focus 4: The Goal Scenario (p. 103 ff.).

It is recommended that you download these pages from the Internet or make copies of the empty form so that you can update your list periodically.

B 5: Values list for material well-being, possessions, wealth

O Security   O Independence

O Money   O Wealth

O Car   O Travel

O House   O Holiday house

O Boat   O Luxury

O Jewellery   O Works of art

O Clothes   O Horse(s)

O Foundation   O Gold

O Gemstones   O Network

O Hobbies   O Insurance

O Shares   O Funds

O Securities   O Properties

O Speculative investments

O _____

O _____

O _____

O _____

O _____

O _____

My current six most important values in the B5 area: Values list for material well-being, possessions, wealth are:

O _____

O _____

O _____

O _____

O _____

O _____

These values are currently ranked:

1. _____

2. _____

3. _____

4. _____

5. _____

6. _____

Date _____

Continuation: Transfer values to an Integrity Wheel with six sectors (see steps 6–9 in section A, p. 89 ff.) and then continue with Focus 4: The Goal Scenario (p. 103 ff.).

It is recommended that you download these pages from the Internet or make copies of the empty form so that you can update your list periodically.

B 6: Values list for evaluation by others, prestige, recognition, social role

O Recognition   O Prestige

O Praise   O Popularity

O Title   O Car(s)

O Being a sponsor   O Clothes

O Respect   O Designer furniture

O Being up with   O Relationships
the latest trends

O Being loved   O Being a patron

O Designer wardrobe

O Being politically active

O Wearing a custom wristwatch

O Knowing important people

O Being referred to in the press / on TV

O Making a contribution to society

O Being part of society

O Supporting the world of ideas

O Being active in an association

O Having an attractive partner

O _____

O _____

My current six most important six values in the B
6 area: Values list for evaluation by others, prestige, recognition, social role are:

O   _____

O   _____

O   _____

O   _____

O   _____

O   _____

These values are currently ranked:

1. _____

2. _____

3. _____

4. _____

5. _____

6. _____

Date _____

*Continuation: Transfer values to an Integrity Wheel with
six sectors (see steps 6–9 in section A, p. 89 ff.) and then
continue with Focus 4: The Goal Scenario (p. 103 ff.).*

*It is recommended that you download these pages from the
Internet or make copies of the empty form so that you can
update your list periodically.*

Overview of values you plan to more strongly actualize in the future:

1. Values overview A: "all life areas"
Here you can record (a maximum of) three values (see steps 7 and 8, p. 242 ff.)

1.

2.

3.

Record only one value for each of the particular life areas:

B 1: Personal growth, personality development

B 2: Profession, career, business

B 3: Personal relationships, friendship, love, partnership, family, home

B 4: Physique, health, sport, games, leisure time, holidays, recuperation

B 5: Material well-being, possessions, wealth

B 6: Evaluation by others, prestige, recognition, social role

(Value 1:)   *means for me*
that

_____

_____

(Value 2:)   *means for me*
that

_____

_____

(Value 3:)   *means for me*
that

_____

_____

(Value 4:)   *means for me*
that

_____

_____

(Value 5:)   *means for me*
that

_____

_____

(Value 6:)   *means for me*
that

_____

_____

_____

Checklist: Goal Scenario

Phase 1: **"What do I WANT?"**

Aspect 1: Make sure you that you are clearly aware of the purpose of achieving your goal

Aspect 2: Establish your goal in writing

Aspect 3: Formulate a self-reference

Aspect 4: Use a word of action that expresses your enthusiasm

Aspect 5: Formulate your goal in the present tense

Aspect 6: Formulate your goal in positive terms (avoid negations!)

Aspect 7: Make the moment of achieving your goal recognizable

Aspect 8: Set a precise date (or one that is as precise as possible) for the realization of your goal

Aspect 9: Remain realistic

Aspect 10: Pay attention to clarity and consequences

Aspect 11: Trusting and letting go: changes are possible at any time

Phase 2: **"What can I, what do I want to, and what should I give?" (see p. 115 f.)**

Phase 3: **The complete Goal Scenario (HAVE and GIVE) (see p. 154 f.)**

Explanatory text on how to best follow these procedures can be found from page 103 - 111.

Appendix 2: A Reward List

We have taken this list from a book published in 1975 (*Sich ändern lernen* (Learn to change yourself) by Frauke Teegen, Anke Grundmann and Angelika Röhrs), partly because it is amusing to see how someone would have treated themselves over 35 years ago, and also because this list contains a range of suggestions that we would never have come up with, even with the best will in the world. And it may be that these possible "rewards" prompt some quite different ideas …

Underline all the items that you would find pleasant and add as many of your own ideas as possible to the list. Keep the list up to date with whatever your present preferences are.

A Foods: candy, ice cream, fruit, cake, nuts, cookies, bread, salad, yoghurt, pudding

B Alcohol-free drinks: water, milk, tea, coffee, soda

C Alcoholic drinks: beer, wine, champagne, spirits

D Meeting men/women who: look good, are intelligent, have a good job, are interestingd

E Problem-solving: crosswords, mathematical exercises, technical problems

F Listening to music: classical, opera, operettas, musicals, jazz, soul, top-40 hits, folk songs

G Making music: singing, piano, flute, violin, guitar, drums

H Watching sports: soccer, athletics, swimming, skiing, car racing, boxing, dancing

I Playing sport: soccer, volleyball, running, swimming, riding, skiing, car racing, boxing, dancing

J   Radio/television: news, drama, entertainment, sit-coms

K   Reading: illustrated, newspapers, crime, novels, adventure stories, biographies, poetry, comics, romance, non-fiction

L   Shopping: CDs, books, foods, clothes, cosmetics, household goods, car accessories

M   Eroticism/sex: looking at naked men/women, touching, flirting, stroking, cuddling, having sex

N   Being praised for your: looks, charm, work, intelligence, physical strength, hobbies, sport, character, morals, understanding for others

O   Peace and relaxation: sleeping, dozing, yoga, meditation

P Being together/talking with: friends, colleagues

Q Going out to a: restaurant, pub, bar, cinema, café, theater, hair salon, club, party

R Health and well-being: shower, bubble bath, massage, sauna

S Feeling happy with yourself because of your: performance, looks, professional conduct, private life

T Being right in: an argument, discussion

U Animals: dogs, cats, birds

V Handiwork/building/craft

X What do you do when you want to console or treat yourself?

Y Who would you hate to lose?

Z For what would you go through anything not to lose?

We have taken this reward list or "confirmation list," as it was originally called, from the following book:

Sich ändern lernen by Frauke Teegen, Anke Grundmann and Angelika Röhrs (with kind permission of Rowohlt Verlag, Reinbeck near Hamburg, Copyright 1975 Rowohlt Taschenbuch)

Appendix 3: Glossary

Affirmation

An affirmation is a powerful, reinforcing confirmation in the form of a statement. It corrects a negative belief and nullifies it. The statement must be positively phrased and may not contain a negation.

Attentiveness

A condition of increased alertness, openness, and concentration in relation to perception, thought, and behavior.

Autotelic

Having itself as its own purpose; doing something for its own sake; an action that has become an end in itself (auto: self, telos: the goal).

Basal Motivation

Some very strong motivational structures developed even before the acquisition of speech.

Basic assumption

Here: a fundamental belief about one's own self, others, relationships to others, and the world. Basic assumptions are SHOULD dimensions; they provide direction in life and have a security and survival function. Usually, they are not actively acknowledged and direct behavior automatically and unconsciously.

Cerebrum

Developmentally, the most recent part of the human brain, in which the higher thought processes take place. The cerebrum (Cortex cerebri) is the highest organ of integration in the central nervous system. The cerebrum (in conjunction with other areas of the brain) is the center of coordination of consciousness, will, intelligence, memory, and learning ability. Below the cerebrum is the limbic system, the source of feelings of pleasure and displeasure.

Change of importance, principle of	As defined by Maslow – new desires gain in perceived importance once lower-priority desires are satisfied.
Charisma	Magnetic personality; charisma is a characteristic of people who are in harmony with their inner values and their vision.
Cognitive dissonance	A condition of inner tension, which is produced by a discrepancy between a person's attitude and his/her actual behavior. Concept describing an emotional state that can be traced back to the fact that perceptions, feelings, and attitudes are incompatible and/or do not accord with earlier experiences.
Commitment, making a commitment	To be strongly dedicated to something; to undertake an obligation; to feel an inner duty to fulfill a promise, come what may.
Compensation strategy	The development of strength from an existing weakness (or even a handicap or impediment). This strategy can liberate tremendous energy.
Complexity	Here: Gain on a personal level through differentiation (increase in knowledge, individualization, specialization) and integration (understanding of the connections, interactions, and network of elements gained through differentiation, connection to other people, institutions and thoughts).
Creative tension	The gap between vision and present reality is the source of creative tension.
Creativity	A creative force that generates new ideas or realigns familiar ideas with one another. An aspect of productive thought expressed when an individual arrives at novel ideas and original solutions fluently and flexibly.

To a large degree, creativity is independent of the kind of achievement demanded by conventional intelligence tests, which essentially are aimed at analytical, convergent thought. Creative processes, by contrast, are characteristic of synthetic, analogous, and divergent thinking. Creative results are to be expected, above all, when an individual has strong, intrinsic motivation.

Detached involvement

A term formulated by Jagdish Parikh to describe the (apparent) contradiction between a strong commitment and the necessary composure; a state of calm engagement.

Differentiation

Increase in knowledge, individualization, specialization; increase of individual elements of a system.

Ecological check

Concept derived from neuro-linguistic programming (NLP). Represents a stage in a process of change in which the question of whether a particular change can be accommodated harmoniously in a person's life is examined.

FLOW

Feeling of happiness; form of happiness over which we have influence; a concept advanced by American psychologist Czickszentmihalyi, describing a generally desirable state achieved in moments of achievement, of overcoming challenges, of a deeper understanding of inter-connectedness, of oneness with yourself and the world.

Freedom

People often define freedom as "free from". But there is also a "freedom for" or a "freedom to," e.g., when you decide in favor of someone or something (by making a commitment to yourself or someone else).

GIVING

Part of the Goal Scenario that describes the things that one is ready to bring or contribute.

Goal	An individual shapes his/her future through a clear formulation of goals. Clear goals are the greatest source of power for personal growth. Philosophy: goals are defined by free, individual choices and decisions, or by social/political decisions and decision-making processes. Goals are projected, future conditions, which may be realized through actions conducive to the planning and implementation of these goals. All intentional actions are determined by goals and substantiated by motives, which attach a value to the prevailing goal such that it is deemed worthy of effort.
Goal Scenario	A concrete, complete representation, in written form, of a desirable future state.
Guided fantasy journey	Text spoken during a relaxed state, which prompts the creation of pictures in the imagination, making it possible to involve the power of the subconscious in the goal-setting process.
Getting	The part of the Goal Scenario that describes the situation that one would like to experience or be a recipient of.
Homeostasis	Regulation of the inner environment through generation of balance and stability.
Imagination exercise	see fantasy journey
Inner calling	see Mission
Integration	Understanding of the relationships, interactions, and network of elements gained through differentiation with the whole, the linkages to and between other people, institutions, and thoughts.
Integrity Wheel	Schematic representation of a person's most important values and their degree of fulfillment.

Late Bloomer	People who find and experience their vision/mission late in life.
Limbic system	Part of the brain that, developmentally speaking, is older than the cerebrum; rapid, automatic reactions stem from the limbic system (e.g., the flight or fight response in stressful situations.) It is in the limbic system that the distinction between feelings of pleasure and displacement are generated. The limbic system evolved from the olfactory brain-center of reptiles and, hence, is also known as the 'reptile brain' (a term more likely to lead to misunderstanding than increased understanding).
Mission	or vocation. Here, referring to the specific contribution of an individual to others and the world. A perception of tasks, which goes beyond the maintenance of one's own biological existence.
Motivation	Driving force, which derives its power from a motive (or more than one motive). From the Latin movere meaning move. The term refers to the powers of a person to purposefully accomplish something specific. Self-motivation refers to the power of an individual to move themselves to an intentional action, largely independently of outside influences.
Motivation, extrinsic	Motivation produced by external incentives.
Motivation, intrinsic	Drive produced by internal values/goals/incentives.
Motivation research	Motivation research aims to determine the sources of human drives.
Plateau phase	Stagnation during the learning process followed by a leap in understanding.

Primary system	Striving towards the satisfaction of physiological needs.
Psychic entropy	Condition of inner tension; feeling of inner confusion.
Purpose the action	*(Merriam-Webster:)* Something that one hopes or intends to accomplish; for which a person or thing is specially fitted or used or for which a thing exists; the reason why something is done or used; the aim or intention of something; the feeling of being determined to do or achieve something; the aim or goal of a person; what a person is trying to do, become, etc.
Resonance	Feeling of harmony between the direction of one's life or situation and one's inner existential core, values, vision/mission; mutual understanding between persons in a communication situation.
Ritual	Rituals are symbolic actions in which particular things are consciously reinforced and recognized in terms of their place in reality. Rituals can be momentous (e.g., weddings) or small, daily habits (e.g., a cup of tea or coffee in the morning).
Secondary system bottleneck orientation	Striving towards synergy, harmony, happiness, resonance, and meaning.
Self attributed motives	Motivational aspects formed after a human has acquired speech.
Self-realization	Aspiration of a person to bring to light his/her talents, abilities, thoughts, ideas, and potential.

Strategy	Utilization of existing resources to achieve the greatest effect. Strengthening strengths: strengths are reinforced by focusing on innate talents and abilities (in contrast to a compensation strategy).
Strategy (bottleneck orientation)	Focus of thoughts and activities on the removal of bottleneck situations. A concept formula ted by Wolfgang Mewes (and Hans Hass) based on patterns of success in nature and economics.
Subconscious	Originally employed by Freud to describe the collective sum of repressed memories and tendencies. Here, the definition is extended to include the parts of ourselves of which we are not consciously aware.
Synapses	[from Greek] Morphologically specialized points in the nervous system that exist between nerve cells (neurons) or between primary sensory cells and other nerve cells or reactive organs (muscle cells, gland cells). Synapses allow for the transfer of nervous excitation from one cell to another.
Synergy	Term derived from psychosynergetics referring to a high degree of integration in an individual.
Transcendence	Growing beyond oneself, perception of supra-individual connectivity of all being.
Unconscious	Originally defined by Freud as the collective sum of repressed memories and tendencies. Here, the definition is extended to include the parts of ourselves of which we are not consciously aware.
Value	Concepts of what a person sees as important in what they bring to the world. An intensely desired condition of feeling; the fundamental basis of a value-oriented life.

Value, attitudinal value	As formulated by Frankl: the possibility of experiencing meaning in the attitude to an imposed destiny.
Value, ultimate value	Ultimate emotional state, as opposed to intermediate values.
Value, intermediate value	Value that serves as a means to reach an ultimate value (e.g., families can impart love, security, refuge, etc.).
Vision	That which a person would like to achieve or receive in life.
Vision, dead	Compulsive images that produce a destruction mental ideal according to the principle of "all or nothing."
Will	Ability of a person to consciously adopt a particular behavior. In traditional psychology, a person's ability to consciously decide for (or against) a particular mental attitude or mode of behavior. The corresponding psychological energy (willpower) differs from pressure or drive, due to its conscious and purposeful character. In modern psychology, terms like desire/want are preferred to the philosophically contentious concept of will.
Wish	Wishes describe an orientation; they are an expression of what is important and valuable to us, and are elicited by unfulfilled values. Wishes can become reality through goals.

Appendix 4: Bibliography

Adrienne, Carol: The Purpose of Your Life, Eagle Brook, New York, 1998

Allen, Marc: The Perfect Life, New World Library, San Rafael, 1992

Allen, Marc: The Type-Z Guide to Success, New World Library, Novato, 2006

Assagioli, Roberto: The act of will. A Guide to Self-Actualisation, David Platts Pub. Co, London 2002

Backerra, Hendrik, Malorny, Christian, Schwarz, Wolfgang: Kreativitätstechniken, Hanser Verlag, Munich 2007

Bateson, Gregory: Steps to an Ecology of Mind: Collected Essays in Anthropology, Psychiatry, Evolution, and Epistemology, University Of Chicago Press, Chicago 2000

Bateson, Gregory: Mind and Nature. A Necessary Unity, Bantam, New York 1988

Böckmann, Walter: Sinnorientierte Leistungsmotivation und Mitarbeiterführung, Ferdinand Enke Verlag, Stuttgart 1980

Bolles, Richard Nelson: What Color is Your Parachute, Ten Speed Press, Berkeley 2004

Buckingham, Marcus, Coffman, Curt: First, Break all the Rules. What the World's Greatest Managers Do Differently, Pocket Books, London 2005

Buckingham, Marcus, Clifton, Donald O.: Now, Discover Your Strengths, Free Press, New York 2001

Castaneda, Carlos: The Teachings of Don Juan: A Yaqui Way of Knowledge, Washington Square Press, Washington 1985

Covey, Stephan R.: The 7 Habits of Highly Effective People, Free Press, New York 1989

Covey, Stephen R.: First Things First, Simon & Schuster, New York/London/Toronto 1994

Crystal, John C., Bolles, Richard N.: Where Do I Go From Here With My Life?, Ten Speed Press, Berkeley 1974

Csikszentmihalyi, Mihaly: Flow: The Psychology of Optimal Experience, Harper & Row, New York 1991

Csikszentmihalyi, Mihaly: The Evolving Self: A Psychology For the Third Millenium, Harper Collins, New York 1993

Csikszentmihalyi, Mihaly: Finding Flow, The Psychology of Engagement With Everyday Life, Harper Collins (BasicBooks), New York, 1997

Csikszentmihalyi, Mihaly: Flow and Education, Flow and Evolution, Flow and Creativity, The NAMTA Journal, Rediscovering Normalization: Deepening the Montessori Experience, Vol. 22, No. 2, Spring 1997

Cube, Felix von: Fordern statt verwöhnen, Piper Verlag, Munich 1998

Ferrucci, Piero: What We May Be, Jeremy P. Tarcher, New York 2004

Foerster, Heinz von, Bröker, Monika: Teil der Welt, Carl-Auer-Systeme Verlag, Heidelberg 2002 (English edition published 2008)

Frankl, Victor: Man's Search for Meaning: An Introduction to Logotheraphy, Pocket Press, Pocket Books 1971

Fritz, Robert: The Path of Last Resistance For Managers, Berrett-Koehler Publishers, San Francisco 1999

Fritz, Robert: Your Life As Art, Robert Fritz Inc. Newfane 2002

Fromm, Erich: Escape of Freedom, Farrar & Rinehart, New York 1941

Gallwey, W. Timothy: The Inner Game of Work. Overcoming Mental Obstacles for Maximum Performance, Texere Publishing, New York/London 2002

Gawain, Shakti: Creative Visualization: Use the Power of Your Imagination to Create What You Want in Your Life, New World Library, Novato 2002

Grossmann, Gustav: The Formula for Success: The Grossmann Method of Self-Rationalization, Thorsons, 1957

Haken, Hermann, Haken-Krell, Maria: Gehirn und Verhalten, Deutsche Verlagsanstalt, Stuttgart 1997

Harris, Thomas A.: I'm Ok, You're Ok, Harper Paperbacks, New York 2004

Hansch, Dietmar: Psychosynergetik, Westdeutscher Verlag, Opladen 1994

Hansch, Dietmar: Evolution und Lebenskunst, Vandenhoeck & Ruprecht, Göttingen 2002

Hansch, Dietmar: Erfolgsprinzip Persönlichkeit, Springer Verlag, 2002

Hill, Napoleon: Think and Grow Rich!, Aventine Press, San Diego 2004

Hillman, James: The Soul's Code: In Search of Character and Calling, Grand Central Publishing, New York 1997

Holzkamp-Osterkamp, Ute: Grundlagen der psychologischen Motivationsforschung, Campus Verlag, Frankfurt/Main 1977

Hugo-Becker, Annegret, Becker, Henning: Motivation. Neue Wege zum Erfolg, C. H. Beck, Munich 1990

Huhn, Gerhard: Kreativität und Schule. Verfassungswidrigkeit staatlicher Regelungen von Bildungszielen und Unterrichtsinhalten vor dem Hintergrund neuerer Erkenntnisse der Gehirnforschung, Verlag für Wissenschaft und Bildung, Berlin 1990

Huhn, Gerhard: Erziehung zur Kreativität, in: Kroker, Eduard J. M. (Hg.), „Erziehung und Bildung – Verspielen wir unsere Zukunftschancen?" Verlag der FAZ, Frankfurt/Main 1998

Huhn, Gerhard: Jenseits der Illusionen, in: „Führung neu verordnen – Perspektiven für Unternehmenslenker im 21. Jahrhundert", PA Consulting und Gabler Verlag, 2007

Kast, Verena: Vom Interesse und Sinn der Langeweile, Walter Verlag, Düsseldorf 2001

Längle, Alfried: Entscheidung (Hg.): Entscheidung zum Sein, V. E. Frankls Logotherapie in der Praxis, Piper Verlag, Munich 1988

Landberg, Max: The TAO of Motivation, Harper Collins Publishers, London 1999

LeBoeuf, Michael: Imageneering. How to Profit From Your Creative Powers, Contemporary Books Inc, Chicago 1982

Leuner, Hanscarl: Lehrbuch des Katathymen Bilderlebens, Huber, Bern 1994

Lewin, Roger: Complexity: Life at the Edge of Chaos, University Of Chicago Press, Chicago 2000

Lynch, Dudley, Kordis, Paul L.: Strategy of the Dolphin, Random House Business Books, London 1989

Malik, Fredmund: Managing, Performing, Living. Effective Management for a New Era, DVA, London 2003

Maslow, Abraham H.: Motivation and Personality, Harper, New York 1954

May, Rollo: Freedom and Destiny, W. W. Norton & Company, New York 1999

Miller, Georg A., Galanter, Eugene, Pribram, Karl H.: Plans and the Structure of Behavior, Holt, Rinehart and Winston, New York 1960

Plakos, Wolfgang: Das Geheimnis des Flow, mvg, Landsberg am Lech 2001

Rheinberg, Falko: Motivation, Kohlhammer Verlag, Stuttgart 2006

Robbins, Anthony: Awaken the Giant Within, Simon & Schuster, New York 1991

Rossi, Ernest Lawrence: Psychobiology of Mind-Body Healing: New Concepts of Therapeutic Hypnosis, W. W. Norton & Company, New York 1993

Scheele, Paul R.: Natural Brilliance, Learning Strategies Corporation, Minnetonka 2001

Schmidbauer, Wolfgang: Alles oder nichts, Rowohlt Taschenbuch Verlag, Reinbek 1999

Schulz von Thun, Friedemann: Miteinander reden 2, Rowohlt Taschenbuch Verlag, Reinbek 1998

Schulz von Thun, Friedemann: Miteinander reden 3, Rowohlt Taschenbuch Verlag, Reinbek 1998

Seiwert, Lothar J.: Wenn Du es eilig hast, gehe langsam, Campus Verlag, Frankfurt/Main 1998

Seiwert, Lothar J.: Life-Leadership. Sinnvolles Selbstmanagement für ein Leben in Balance, Campus Verlag, Frankfurt/Main 2001

Seiwert, Lothar J.: Das Bumerang-Prinzip: Mehr Zeit fürs Glück, Gräfe und Unzer, Munich 2002 (www.bumerang-prinzip.de)

Seligman, Martin: Learned Optimism, Alfred Knopf, New York 1990

Seligman, Martin: Authentic Happiness, The Free Press, New York 2002

Senge, Peter: The Fifth Discipline: The Art & Practice of The Learning Organization, Currency, New York 2006

Sprenger, Reinhart K.: Das Prinzip Selbstverantwortung, Campus Verlag, Frankfurt/Main 1995

Sprenger, Reinhart K.: Mythos Motivation, Campus Verlag, Frankfurt/Main 1992

Stephan, Naomi: Finding Your Life Mission, Stillpoint Publishing, Walpole, 1989

Stone, Hal, Stone, Sidra: Partnering: A New Kind of Relationship, New World Library, Novato 2000

Stone, Hal, Stone, Sidra: Embracing Ourselves, New World Library, Novato 1998

Teegen, Frauke, Grundmann, Anke, Röhrs, Angelika: Sich ändern lernen, Rowohlt Verlag, Reinbek 1975

Varela, Francisco J.: Kognitionswissenschaft – Kognitionstechnik, Suhrkamp TB Verlag, Frank-furt/Main 1993

Vester, Frederic: Denken, Lernen, Vergessen, DTV, Stuttgart 1998

Watzlawick, Paul, Weakland, John H., Fisch, Richard: Lösungen, Hans Huber Verlag, Bern/Göttingen/Toronto 1992

Winograd, Terry, Flores, Fernando: Understanding Computers and Cognition, Greenwood Publishing Group, Westport 1986

Wolff, Lorenz, Frank, Johanna: Berufszielfindung und Umsetzungstrategie, GABAL, Speyer 1992

Zdenek, Marilee: The Right-Brain Experience, Mc Graw-Hill Book Company, New York 1983

Note of Thanks

As stated at the outset, the material in this book has been drawn from many years of practical experience and from personal failures and successes that have come during expansive and regressive periods and turbulent and peaceful times. It would be remiss of us not to admit that in terms of content, we have been able to stand on the shoulders of men and women who have contemplated the issues raised here for longer and more deeply than we have, and in this sense, we see ourselves as their interpreters. We are certainly not claiming to present something completely new here; our aim has been to show that the things we consider valuable can also be experienced and developed by others, and in doing so, we wanted to express these ideas in accessible language and as a series of highly practical steps.

Our seminar participants and coaching clients have helped show us what is feasible in this respect, and we would like to thank them first and foremost. Without them the idea for this book would never have taken shape and we would not have learned what we are presenting here. We would also like to thank the authors and teachers who have made our work possible, and who are referred to in the preceding bibliography.

Every person with whom we have had contact, exchanged ideas or established a friendship during the genesis of this book has contributed in his or her own unique way to our work, sometimes with and sometimes without his or her knowledge. We would like to express out heartfelt thanks to all of you for your inspiration, ideas, incentives, and encouragement; unfortunately you are too numerous to name. Furthermore, we would like to thank all those people who have provided us with concrete help in the form of criticism, acknowledgement, advice, and encouragement.

The Authors

Dr. Gerhard Huhn is a leading expert supporting people in transferring the findings of scientific brain research into their daily routines. By »strengthen the strengths« he helps to improve and enhance learning processes, creativity, self-motivation, leadership and entrepreneurial thinking. His focus is to expand the understanding and the practical use of the Flow-Concept of Prof. Mihaly Csikszentmihalyi by applying the »3-Dimensional-Flow Space« (design of future scenarios by integration of strengths and values). Dr. Huhn worked with companies like BMW, Kraft Foods, Unilever, Henkel, Vodafone etc. but also with small business entrepreneurs, startups and individuals. His professional life includes after a career as Vice President of Sales in a direct sales company eight years being a lawyer in his own law consulting company, ten years as an independent publisher and now 30 years as consultant, coach and management trainer (partly parallel to the other activities). Since many years he worked parallel as a visiting lecturer in national and international universities and published several books and articles.
You can contact him at gerhard.huhn@googlemail.com / www.gerhardhuhn.com

Hendrik Backerra runs his consultancy focusing on organizational development, creating healthy leadership-cultures and supporting transformation processes in cooperation worldwide. Previously he worked as an expert for organizational development at McKinsey&Company and as engagement manager for IBM Global Services. He studied industrial economy and is a certified coach. He and his team are focusing on innovative, inspiring and impactful interventions which help the organizations to better deal with the rapid change in our current economy and integrating the strategic needs with personal human development. Topics range from transformational leadership, consultative selling, innovation to personal effectiveness. His expertise is regulary used by clients from the fields of finance, production, services and include international cooperation's, start-ups, non-governmental organizations as well as public services.

He is author of several books and writes article about his latest insights.

You can reach Hendrik Backerra and his team at change@hendrikbackerra.de
www.hendrikbackerra.de

www.ingramcontent.com/pod-product-compliance
Lightning Source LLC
Chambersburg PA
CBHW020153200326
41521CB00006B/349